Aberdeenshire Library and Information Service
www.aberdeenshire.gov.uk.libraries
Renewals Hotline 01224 661511

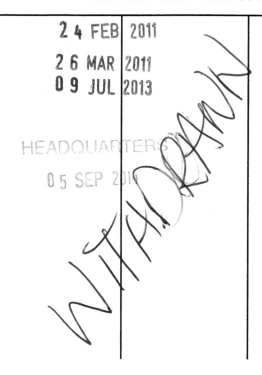

A WHISPER FROM AN ANGEL

How I became a bridge between
heaven and earth

Christine Holohan

with Vera McHugh

Previously published in 2006 as 'A Voice from the Grave.'

This new and revised edition published in 2009
by Maverick House Publishers, Office 19, Dunboyne Business
Park, Dunboyne, Co. Meath, Ireland.

www.maverickhouse.com
email: info@maverickhouse.com

ISBN 978-1905379-65-1

5 4 3 2 1

Printed and bour

The paper used i
forests. For every
renewing natural

The moral rights
All rights reserve

A CIP catalogue record for this book is available from the British
Library.

CONTENTS

- ACKNOWLEDGEMENTS -

I WOULD LIKE to pay tribute to some very special people who came into my life as a direct result of the Jacqui Poole case, notably Mr. Montague Keen, and his colleague and friend Mr. Guy Lyon Playfair, both members of the Society for Psychical Research. Both men have proved invaluable in my search for answers in the spirit world.

My thanks must also be extended to Detective Tony Batters and his colleague Detective Andy Smith, who believed my story through all those years. Both Tony and Montague have passed on, within two weeks of each other. It was strange how all our lives could become entwined with the evidence of the survival of the spirit after death.

Monty's dear widow, Veronica, remains very close to me and I continue to pass messages from her loved one. In the bridge of love that spans the two worlds, Tony has passed on guidance and love to his widow Ann and family, and I would like to thank them for their support and assistance in writing this book. I, for one, feel very honoured to have met such wonderful people who not only became friends but who were in a position to validate my story.

I sent a copy of my book to Detective Constable Andy Smith who was the other officer, with Detective Constable Tony Batters, who investigated the murder of Jacqui Poole. It was lovely to speak to Andy after such a long time and also to hear him say that the interview conducted back in Ruislip all those years ago changed his life forever.

I had told him some details about his life and in truth when I told him that he was to be transferred to another police station, naturally he was sceptical. That was until the information that I had given him came to pass within a matter of days. We keep in touch now and remain friends to this day. I was able to console his wife when her father passed, which gave her great relief.

Special thanks must also go to Vera McHugh for all her help, and to her brother Brian, and her late mother Alice.

Many thanks to all at Maverick House Publishers, and to all the people I have worked with over the years.

Christine Holohan, September 2009.

- DEDICATION -

This book is dedicated to my mother Kathleen and my late father Thomas, my sister Mary, my nephew Canice, my niece Lorraine, my brother Peter and my late brother Martin, my late cousin Kathleen and all my extended family, for recognising I had a gift and accepting me for who I am.

I would also like to give a special dedication to the memory of Jacqui Poole; an incredible person.

- FOREWORD -

by Barbara Kendall-Davies

THERE IS A great deal of ignorance about clairvoyance, and I was unaware of its existence until I heard two colleagues talking about mediums they had met in America. What they had to say was interesting but I could not identify with it because I had no experience of such things.

Unknown to me, fate was waiting in the wings to uncover a new world. Seemingly by chance, I met Christine Holohan at my son's school fete in 1982. She was giving her services in aid of school funds, allotting ten minutes to each client. At my son's insistence, I queued to see her, and little realised that I was embarking on the most wonderful journey of discovery.

My father-in-law had died suddenly the previous summer, followed by an uncle three months later; I was away on both occasions. Christine knew nothing of this, but she brought them both to me, and she was so accurate in her description of looks and personality that I had to take her seriously. She also described some splendid buildings in detail, although she didn't know where they were. I recognised them as being in Munich where my work took me each summer for five years, and I happened to be returning there the following week. It's strange how we seem to want to catch people out, and when Christine said that my father-in-law and uncle had found their red setter, I told her that couldn't be as they had never had such a dog, but when I told my husband about it, he recognised the dog as Paddy, a pet they had had when he was a toddler. It had been dead for over thirty years.

Christine was tuning into something real, but I couldn't understand how she did it. I had to learn more, so I became a member of the College of Psychic Studies in London. Her things opened up remarkably, and my own psychic awareness developed incredibly. Christine was my catalyst and my family and many others have indirectly benefited from her gifts.

Over the past twenty-two years my knowledge and understanding has deepened, and I treat psychic matters with respect. Such energies are not to be played with lightly, but they can teach us a Science of Life, hardly guessed at by the majority of people. One day I will write the story of Christine, myself, and a third person, who came to us from another realm, because it is a remarkable one, and full of wonders. Shakespeare was quite right when he said, 'There are more things in heaven and earth, Horatio, than are dreamt of in your philosophy.'

- INTRODUCTION -

I CAN'T INTRODUCE this book without mentioning William Roach who plays the beloved Ken in 'Coronation Street', a popular soap drama on British television. I would like to thank William for his friendship and encouragement after he read *A Voice from the Grave*, which was the first edition of *A Whisper from an Angel*. It is strange when I think of how I came to know him.

After the hectic time that followed the publication and launch of the first book I recall one evening having a feeling that I should send my book to him. The more I thought about it the more amazed I became. I did not know anything about William Roach, only that he happens to be one of the stars of 'Coronation Street'. How could I possibly think of sending him a copy and what was it that was prompting me so strongly? As I had no personal knowledge of the man and his likes and dislikes when it came to reading material, I could only come to one conclusion: that it was the angels who were interfering and urging me to send him a copy of the book.

I relented, sent it off and forgot all about it until late in the autumn of 2006. Shortly after I had sent it to William I received a lovely, warm letter from him telling me how much he had enjoyed reading the book and inviting me to come over to meet him. He was fascinated with the story and amazed at how a spirit had reached out to me across that great divide that keeps our loved ones apart from us. He was very anxious to talk to me.

I went to England with my sister, Mary, in June 2007 and can quite honestly say that we were welcomed royally by William and the cast of 'Coronation Street'. He came to greet us at our hotel and we walked with him to the studio. It was as if we had known each other forever. He is a deeply spiritual man, hence his desire to meet me and share his beliefs with me. He has had a belief in angels all his life. We had a most enlightening conversation about angels and spirit guides, particularly the Native American Indian Guide who brings wisdom and healing.

It was an amazing visit to the studio and to arrive as the guest of someone the calibre of William Roach is very special and will remain with me for a very long time.

It was so exciting to meet the cast face to face; they really are such lovely people. One of the actors,

Sally, was celebrating her fortieth birthday and filming was in progress. I met her screen husband and other members of the cast. It was fun to see the sets I had become familiar with as a fan of the show, and William made sure to show us the vast wardrobe. We were entertained to tea in his dressing room and afterwards with some champagne to celebrate Sally's birthday. We keep in touch and I was in contact with him recently when his wife died.

It was through William that I came to meet Lorna Byrne, the author of 'Angels in my Hair'. I gave her a copy of my book when I met her in Maynooth, County Kildare. I swear she had wings even though I could not see them. She had an amazing aura and presence about her and is so very humble. She brought the same essence that I remember as a child when the angels came to me. I was totally in awe of her. Only once before had I experienced that same feeling of being loved and I knew that I was in the presence of an angel.

After the publication of the first edition of the book it was a rollercoaster of excitement. Our launch in Dublin was attended by family and friends and, to tell the truth, lots of policemen. It seemed that they were very interested in the Jacqui Poole story. In Portlaoise, we had the biggest ever book launch attended by over 300 guests in Jim Tynan's famous restaurant, The Kitchen. This was followed by another in Athy, County Kildare. The book is still in demand and engagements are still coming in three years down the road and will continue to do so. Japanese television sent a crew over to record an interview with me and then made a documentary about my encounter with Jacqui Poole.

Canadian Film made another feature on the Jacqui Poole story. I have been interviewed on many television programmes and radio stations, not to mention newspapers and magazines. I hope you enjoy this updated version of the book, which includes more about my own background, upbringing and my continuous experiences with angels.

Christine Holohan.

- CHAPTER 1-

THE ANGELS FIRST came to me when I was little more than a baby. I spent a lot of time in my cot, it doubled as a playpen. I can remember it well; it was wooden and not filled with as many toys as children have today. I did not need my cot bursting with toys, as I had the company of angels who knew exactly when to come to me.

My heavenly playmates came floating into my room, filling every inch of space with their presence. I was enveloped in their warmth and sense of fun, but more than anything, I was filled with a magical feeling I can only describe as unconditional love. They would come like a swarm of butterflies on a magnificent rainbow of colour, the like of which I have not seen since. They weren't loud; I could only hear the gentle fluttering of their wings as they busied themselves dancing and playing. I had no idea who my friends were or that I had been chosen as a playmate for the angels.

The first thing I would notice was the clouds; they came, swirling and dancing into every corner of my room, before settling softly around me. Joy rained down on me as they slowly surrounded my little cot and a golden light would break through the colours as my little angels appeared.

When they came they had an air of playfulness about them, and also an energy of unconditional love, just for me. I spent many happy hours playing with my angels, but like every child with something new, I eventually tired of my friends.

Sometimes I would be tired and not in the mood to play with them, and I remember telling them to go away. I was approaching the age of three and like most other children, longed to explore horizons beyond the confines of my cot and my bedroom. I had taken my amazing friends for granted and in my efforts to reach out for new experiences I tired of my precious companions.

Not realising that I was about to stop seeing them, I stumbled on. My special friends, knowing much more than I did, allowed me to go on my journey. They told me they would go, but that they would stay with me even though I may not see them anymore, and they would remain with me until the end of time, to love and protect me. Through my life they have done just this.

They kept their solemn promise that they would be with me forever, but with the one condition that

I would never see them again. It was as if I knew what they were thinking and feeling, I remember knowing that a promise had been made with a condition attached, and I knew deep inside they would be with me forever.

It is said that babies and very young children can see much more than adults; this is because their spirits are pure and unblemished. As we grow older our senses become blurred and we are less inclined to focus on anything beyond our immediate surroundings. This other world where angels dwell is so close to ours, yet might be a million miles away.

I was born on Sunday, 21 December; the winter solstice, a very auspicious day to come into this world, and at the very same time that the winter sun floods the Neolithic burial tomb at Newgrange in County Meath. I was the third child born after a long gap to my parents Kathleen and Thomas Holohan. I was not to know for a long time that I had been blessed with the gift of second sight but my grandmother on my father's side, Mary Ann, who herself had psychic tendencies, remarked to my mother as she carried me down to the church for my christening that I was an old soul because I was very alert, smiling and looking all around me. I never crawled as a baby, but just took off walking at less than a year.

Most children accept the events that occur in their lives as normal and find it hard to imagine life being anything other than what they have experienced. This holds true for at least the first eight years, then slowly events outside the home impact on their senses and the realisation dawns that things are different outside their own four walls. In my childhood, though we weren't so well off, we were warm and well looked after and always well dressed, which in those days wasn't easy. I wanted to play outside like the rest of the children in my home town of Stradbally, County Laois, but I had not been granted perfect health. I struggled for many a year and spent more time in bed listening to the other children running and playing while I had to stay inside.

As a child I thought that everyone was the same, and believed that they could see and sense the same things I could. I presumed that everybody had special playmates when they were very young, who circled their cot in a swirl of colours and light, but I was different, different in so many ways from my friends and also my siblings. To look at I appeared just like any other child and could generally pass unnoticed in a crowd.

As I grew older I learnt that not everyone had seen angels and not everyone believed in them, nor would they believe me if I spoke about them, so I learnt to keep my gift hidden, secret. However, I always kept in touch with my psychic side and I allowed my angels to guide me throughout my life.

It is one thing being blessed and quite another to be entirely unaware of the fact.

It is only now as an adult, remembering the events that marked me out as different from my friends and those around me, I am convinced that I have indeed been truly blessed.

🍀 🍀 🍀 🍀 🍀

It was by no means fanciful thinking that I might have had a sixth sense, because there was a history of it in my family and there were many stories that seemed to prove it. My mother, for instance, was always very sure of signs in her dreams. One night she dreamt that she was in a crowd of people, all wearing black, and a nun walked over to her with an umbrella. One week later my cousin died and at the funeral a nun walked straight over to her and offered her shelter from the rain under her umbrella.

My father too, seemed to have the same uncanny ability. I think he inherited it from his mother. One night he dreamt Granny was giving out to my Uncle Paddy, and when he went to see her he asked why she was giving out. The poor woman was convinced he had been hiding outside the window listening to them, because he was right.

My grandmother predicted her own death. One night when we were all sitting around the fire she said: 'This time next year I'll be gone,' and exactly one year later she died. It seems that the gift of second sight also runs in the extended family. A cousin of mine told his brother one day to 'mind the high wires'. One week into his new job, they day after the warning, the brother was electrocuted and killed when the trailer attached to his lorry hit electrical wires above him.

My cousin Kathleen also tended to be psychic. When new houses were about to be built in the area around Stradbally, the foundations were just being put in place, but she knew exactly which one she would end up in. She also used to get what she described as a 'bad feeling' every time she passed a certain place on the road to Portlaoise, predicting that someone was going to be killed there. This turned out to be horribly true.

STRADBALLY IS KNOWN as 'the home of steam' due to its annual Steam Rally, and today is probably best known for its music festival, Electric Picnic, but it is full of history. To me, my brothers Peter and Martin, and my sister Mary, the village represented our universe as children, and the place still holds the key to my identity. It is where I feel at home, and is simply full of memories; some good and some bad. It is, in essence, a central part of my life, and indeed a central part of this story. It is where I have experienced most joy, and most tragedy, and where the 'gift' of a medium can most clearly be seen to have a darker side that contrasts starkly with the good and the light and can become as much a curse.

For me, the most important aspect of Stradbally was, and still is what locals refer to as 'The Hall', or sometimes as 'Cosby's'. The Cosby's are synonymous with the village, having been landlords there for centuries. Their grounds lie behind wonderful specimen trees that have been planted over hundreds of years. The land spans about 500 acres of parkland, and because I was always a friend, well-known to the family, I have always been allowed to wander through its vast expanse. The magic that this unspoilt landscape brought to me and my young friends resembled an 'Alice in Wonderland' arena, which has lasted all through my life, even to the present day. I love the land. If I am sad, all I have to do is imagine myself back in that time and space, and peace and tranquillity are instantly restored. It was here that my first real vision, since the angels, happened. I was only seven years old at the time.

My sister Mary, and some friends and I, all decided to have a picnic and afterwards we played the usual games like hide and seek. There was an old house there with a garden, known locally as Bingham's, and a gardeners' lodge, and when I looked over I saw an old woman dressed in Victorian clothes holding a lantern. There were children following her, all dressed in similar clothes. They also wore long dresses and little bonnets. There wasn't really anything spectral or ghostly about them; they just looked like a woman and some children wearing old-fashioned clothes, but it was this that interested me, so I kept my eyes on them. I remember thinking it strange that the woman carried a lantern, even though it was daytime. They just walked around the house, the lady with the lantern out front and the children behind, then they simply disappeared.

I do not remember telling my friends about what I had seen because I imagined that they had also seen the lady with the children and I thought no more about it. But this would not be the last vision I would have at 'The Hall', and though I had many more joyous times there, it would also come to be filled with darker memories for me when I grew older and my life changed. The house and surrounding estate were said to be haunted, and many people were a bit afraid of the house once it got dark, but it never bothered me.

I was a wild and fearless child and took great delight in seeing the adults being scolded from the pulpit at sermons, and having to listen; such was the power of the Church back then. I was once caught by the parish priest doing my own impression of a fire-and-brimstone ritual up on the altar, but it didn't bother me. I believed passionately in the freedom to express myself and did not feel scared or ashamed by my behaviour. Sermons on the Devil and the preaching about the flames of Hell instilled in me a firm belief in the existence of an afterlife, and though as I matured I would form my own opinions, this idea stayed with me, though not in such a dramatic way. Today sermons are all about love and tolerance and I think this is much better.

At times it was fun for me to have second sight, and at other times it was a curse—and this idea has continued with me into my adult life. I was perhaps 12 when I discovered I could read the odd teacup and things like that were all about fun and games to me. I didn't take it seriously, but I became very popular all of a sudden and had a lot of friends.

Some premonitions were not personal and, as a result, they were just a bit strange rather than upsetting. One night I could clearly hear the sound of the popular singer Jim Reeves singing downstairs, so I called down to my mother to see if the radio was on, and that I could hear the words to 'Put Your Sweet Lips a Little Closer to the Phone'. She called back up that there was no radio on and to hurry up and go to sleep. The next morning the tragic news of Reeves' death was announced on the radio, and my mother gave me a very strange look.

But I also had premonitions that came to me without warning, and what made them so awful, so unbearable, was that there was nothing I could do about them. I couldn't help what I saw, and I didn't know exactly what my visions meant until it was too late. They just left me distraught and upset, and wishing I didn't have any kind of special ability or sixth sense; that I could just be a normal girl with a normal life.

I continued to have premonitions at this young age. I was too young to know what they were or what was happening to me back then. I dreamt that my uncle had come to the house to tell my father that his sister, Aunt Maggie, had died. I had seen her myself a week before, down at my Aunt Molly's, and had experienced a strange feeling that I would never see her again. I woke up after my dream to hear my uncle's voice in the house. My father was going down the stairs to him and I called out that Aunt Maggie was dead. My outburst was followed by a strange silence because it was true.

I was great friends with a boy named Joe who used to come to Stradbally every summer, and I was heartbroken when he came one year with the news that his family were moving to England. Two further summers came and went and I missed him a lot, but then one night I woke suddenly to see a young man standing over my bed with his arms folded. He was wearing a white shirt and a grey short-sleeved jumper. I called out to my brother Martin, because I thought it was him, walking in his sleep like he often did. When he answered me sleepily from the comfort of his own bed, I knew it wasn't him, but when I looked up again the boy was gone. A couple of days later we received some very bad news in a letter. My friend Joe, who had been only 14 years old, was dead. My mother showed me the photograph of Joe that came with the letter, and I immediately recognised the young man who had stood above my bed. He looked exactly the same as he had done the night I saw the figure. After that incident though, the angels and the spirits seemed to leave me alone for a while, and I saw nothing out of the ordinary, living a normal life for a period. I guess the angels needed a rest.

The worst premonitions I experienced concerned my brother Martin. At one stage I started to have terrible dreams about him. On three occasions I dreamt of how he would die—the dreams were always the same. I would walk past a derelict building that had a rope hanging in it, but I always kept on going, refusing to see any further. Martin took his own life years later at the age of 30. I have often been asked why I didn't say something to him back then, but what could I have said as a young girl to her younger brother? I guess I just didn't want to acknowledge what was the worst possible thing in the world for me, and my young mind just wasn't equipped to cope with it, so I tried to forget about it and hoped it would go away.

Martin and I were nearly the same age and I have many fond memories of him when we were both much younger; most of them centre around The Hall. But just as with my ability, this place came to be a place of light and dark, of happiness and sadness for me. It was just wonderful walking around the grounds; pure magic, but this was also the place where my brother committed suicide, and the knowledge of this will never fade.

My gift affected every part of my life. I became restless, and after I left school, I travelled around, from Dublin to the Isle of Man, back to Dublin and then finally England, moving from job to job. By the time I had hit my teenage years, I guess I was a little scared of my ability, and wanted to keep some sort of distance from home, where I imagined this sense was at its strongest. The Hall had become a central part of the consciousness that filled my youth with joy but also left me with a strong sense of a beyond, of the power to see things others could not. Even then, in my subconscious, I guess I didn't know if it was a gift or a curse, but there were certainly some things I didn't really want to be able to see.

❧ ❧ ❧ ❧ ❧

Everyone has an angel who cares for us and guides us. This is our guardian angel, and as we progress through life we receive more angels to help us on our way. These angels might be the spirits of those who have passed and have a special interest in us. Life is a journey and as we come to different periods in our lives we receive all the help we need. Sadly not everyone is in tune with their angels, and the suggestion they do exist and are here to help us is frequently met with total disbelief.

Angels work in mysterious ways and believing in angels is not confined to a particular religion. If they want to make you move in a certain direction, you will receive messages. However, you will not for a moment believe you are actually receiving messages from an angel, most likely you will put it down to a sudden thought or a brainwave that has just occurred to you.

I call on my angels to help in my everyday life. I had a beautiful cat one time and she became very ill. I prayed earnestly to my angels for their help before I brought her to the vet. My vet knew me very well as I have several cats and was a constant visitor to his clinic. On this occasion he was trying to tell me gently that there really was nothing he could do for her. All the time I was mentally storming heaven and the angels for a reprieve for Tibbies. As I was handing her over to the vet, out of nowhere a small white feather floated down, landing on the ground between us. That time I got my miracle and Tibbies was with me for another six months before she died. I was very grateful, as I had not been ready to say goodbye to her.

I gradually realised that I couldn't and shouldn't stop from using my gift on a daily basis, and I became less afraid as time went on. I started to help people to communicate with the other side by using the angels as a medium.

I believe I should demystify the words 'clairvoyant', 'medium' and 'psychic' in order to make understanding my story easier. A medium is quite simply a mediator; one who can communicate between earth and the spirit world. A psychic can give advice, guidance and also predict the future. A clairvoyant is one who is both a psychic and a medium. Rather than using scientific or over-technical jargon to detail my abilities, 'a bridge between heaven and earth' is a nicer way of explaining what I do. I help console those who mourn their loved ones who have died. With my gift I am able to bring them closer and ease their pain.

I can also pass on vital information from those who have departed to those in need of answers and information. In recent times I have been called on by the police in England to assist them in locating missing people. I have also worked on cases in Ireland at the request of families and have had my share of success. Times have changed and people are more open to working with mediums now.

Many years ago, though, it was sometimes difficult to convince people that I was telling the truth, until I finally proved beyond any doubt that I could see and converse with those who had passed on. A horrific crime committed just a mile or so away from my house thrust me into an extraordinary situation, and a completely unique and terrifying experience: the murder victim came to me for help. The British Police have openly stated that my contribution to their investigation was both vital and beyond doubt, and that they firmly believe the information I gave them was indisputably real and could only have come from the person who had died.

In all my years growing up I never thought that I would have to explain my life's work to anybody beyond my immediate family and close friends.

However, the death of the young woman called Jacqui Poole changed my life forever, and left me obliged to tell the story of how it all came about.

- CHAPTER 2-

I AWOKE FROM the depths of sleep so quickly that I knew something wasn't right. The room was dark except for the dim blue light burning at the side of my bed, lit earlier to help me meditate. I looked around me, trying to get accustomed to the near darkness, when I realised I wasn't alone. There was someone there, someone standing at the foot of my bed.

My senses were at fever pitch and I was paralysed with fear. My mind was racing, trying to understand this level of fear and what was going on. Eventually my eyes began to see shapes in the twilight, and in an instant the knowledge and the certainty that someone was present was overpowering. With that feeling came a rush of panic that swept over every fibre of my being and it was then I really saw her.

There was an outline of a figure, hidden by the shadows, looking at me, but as I peered into the gloom at the end of my bed the outline became clearer. It was a woman; young and beautiful, with blonde hair down to her shoulders. She was very pretty, but there was something upsetting about her and the intensity of her stare made me shake. As she moved closer to me, I sensed a deep need in her, reaching out to me.

There was such an air of sadness about her that I instinctively knew she meant no harm. The only thing I could feel towards her that night was compassion—she seemed so troubled. The tension rushing through me eased a little as this wraith-like figure sat at the foot of my bed and I realised that she was here for a reason. She wasn't a premonition or a curse, a gift or a blessing. She had an air about her of one calling on official business. I found that reassuring, and strangely curious. She seemed to be fidgeting nervously with her hands while looking down at me. She looked upset and confused as I heard her speak for the first time.

'Help me.'

Her voice seemed to float around the room, like a slow, cold echo, bringing me to a place inside myself where everything felt freeze-framed. Everything about her arrested me and even though she was dead, at that moment she had more life in her than I did.

I promised her I would do whatever I could. Her relief was palpable and although I had agreed to help her I had no real idea what was going on. She moved from the foot of my bed and came closer to me, and I detected a faint smell of perfume from her. I could sense she was a warm and caring person and I was not afraid. It felt like she looked straight into my soul and, with a look of immense sadness and desperation, she inched closer still and pleadingly asked me to help her again, saying: 'I have been murdered.'

Those stark words hung there between us, intensifying the atmosphere.

'Will you help me? I have been murdered.'

As long as I live I will never forget these words. They haunted me then and they continue to haunt me today because I became friends, if you will, with this ghostly entity. I got used to having her around in the end, and I think we could have been friends if I'd met her as a person, under normal circumstances. To have made this connection with somebody who was denied their very existence so early in their life was very saddening.

I was a 22-year-old woman from a small town in County Laois, Ireland who was now living in England, and though I had gained a reputation as a gifted medium, and had a regular group of clients, this was nothing like anything I had ever experienced before. Who was this woman? Why had she come to me? I was used to helping people in my own way, easing people through loss and grief, showing them the way forward, providing comfort, but I wasn't sure what I could do here.

People came to me for many reasons. Some of them had suffered trauma or loss and longed to make contact with loved ones who had left them behind. At times a word of comfort through a spirit helped to ease their pain. This particular weekend had been very busy for me, with people calling for readings, some looking for guidance in life, job opportunities, or indeed many of whom had lots of problems, each one looking for comfort and understanding. But this was something completely different. After the various events that had taken place over the weekend at my home it was almost a relief to find a ghost standing at the foot of my bed. For the last few days I had been waiting for something to happen.

From Friday evening I had started to notice unusual happenings in the flat that I could not relate to. An atmosphere of increasing gloom and depression had settled around me and I knew that something was wrong, but I couldn't tell exactly what it was. I felt upset, but I didn't know where to start looking for an answer to this situation. I began to phone around my friends, checking to see if all was well with them, and with bemused replies they all reassured me that they were fine. This sense of foreboding was so intense and strong that I rang my family in Ireland, but everybody there was fine too and I tried to forget about it.

Saturday morning was no better, and in fact, if anything, the sense of gloom was now all-encompassing and could not be shaken off. This was far more than just a feeling of unease. There was a presence around me; I didn't know exactly what it was but I knew it was troubled. I wondered if it could be connected to a previous sitting with a client, as sometimes spirits lingered for a while. I hoped it was simply this, and I tried to go about my day, but the feeling of someone or something settling around me continued and at one stage on Saturday night I thought I heard someone coming up the hallway. I called out to my sister Mary, who was in bed, and my nephew Canice; both were asleep at the time so there was no reply. I slept fitfully and awoke to the sound of someone banging the bathroom door. I sat up and called out to Mary, who had heard nothing and suggested it was my imagination.

With the coming of morning there was no relief. I had not slept properly all weekend because I kept hearing footsteps, doors opening and closing, and had this ever-present gloom hanging all around me. This feeling of unease continued and I was convinced that something dreadful had happened. It was really getting to me, and it was made worse by the fact I couldn't do anything about it. I hated feeling like this; knowing, just knowing that something was wrong, but having no way of knowing what it was or what to do about it.

I went into the village on Monday morning and overheard two women talking about a young woman by the name of Jacqueline Poole, who had been murdered in the area. I froze. I could not bear to listen. I remember an awful, cold feeling coming over me. I thought perhaps that this was what was wrong with me. I could hear someone call me, but when I looked there was no one there. I went home, very upset, because I thought I was going mad.

Mary thought that I was having a nervous breakdown. Doom and gloom followed me everywhere on Monday. It consumed me. No matter how many times I opened the windows to allow the passage of fresh air into our home this terrible sensation was clinging to the very walls. That evening I felt someone come closer to me. I decided to try and meditate; this was a sure way of settling my mind before sleep. I was drifting off to sleep when suddenly I knew someone was with me in my room, someone was tugging at the end of my bed. From experience, I knew there was a spirit trying to come through and at this stage, because I was so tormented from lack of sleep, I asked straight away, 'Are you Jacqui Poole?' The lights flashed on and off, so I had my answer. I asked if she was Jacqui Poole again and I heard a voice answer, 'Jacqui Hunt', before it suddenly went away. Once more, all was quiet, and I was left alone with my thoughts.

Later that night she returned, cursing and swearing about her murderer. I could not see her but I sensed her presence and heard her angry words. I felt I could not take much more so I ran into my sister's room, covered my head with the duvet and tried to sleep. Somehow, I managed to doze off, but the tugging at the end of the bed started again a while later, and was very insistent, so much so that Mary and I both woke up to see our gas fire steadily burning the end of the blankets. I interpreted this as an omen. The spirit had protected me. I knew then that I had to help this woman, as she had surely saved us, but I didn't know what I could do.

On Tuesday night I awoke and could see a white line like the outline of a person standing beside my bed. I looked up, frightened. Part of me wanted to bury my head in the blankets, but the other part felt I had to know what was going on. It wasn't the spirit that disturbed me—I had seen enough of them in my life already—but the fact that she was so troubled filled me with dread. I turned away because in the end I was too afraid to face her.

The next day, the same horrible, eerie feeling returned to my flat. At one point I felt something brush past me like a breeze, and this continued all day. She was trying to come through. Looking back, I think that maybe I was scared and not as responsive as I should have been at first, but that night it was very quiet, and everyone was asleep, except me. Now, here I was talking to a woman who had been dead for several days, who was asking me to help her. I became increasingly frustrated with her and with me and in the quiet of the night I decided to have it out with her. I knew she was there so I said to her: 'You're in my room again, Jacqui!'

I was almost accusing her of this, as I felt like I was caught in the middle of a nightmare, someone else's nightmare, and self-doubt was creeping anxiously inside me. She told me that she wasn't in my life to make things awkward for me, but that she needed my help, and began to tell me her story.

- CHAPTER 3 -

'WILL YOU HELP me?' she asked again. She seemed so frightened and helpless, so in my mind I promised I would do whatever I could. Sensing her unspoken doubt, I voiced my promise. I could feel her relief. It was as if our senses were in tune. I could feel her worries and fears as if they vibrated somewhere deep within my very soul. She sat closer, and the warmth of her personality enveloped me. I was no longer frightened, just waiting.

She moved closer, and whispered again: 'I've been murdered. Will you help me?' The words sent shivers down my spine, and questions started to fly around in my head, but I didn't need to utter a word because she was in my very mind with me. She leaned closer still, and nodded: 'Yes, I do want you to tell the police I know who killed me and I want everyone to know. I want justice.'

I felt nervous about going to the police; I wondered if they would think I was crazy. I was born psychic, but apart from my family, a few close friend and my few clients, my gift was a closely guarded secret. This was a murder case and I wasn't in the habit of telling everyone I met that I had just been visited by the ghost of a murder victim. Things don't work like that.

In addition, I felt myself worry a little about my own sanity and my perception of what was going on here. Would the police have been right to think I was crazy? Naturally I found doubts in myself, in my abilities, and in my relevance to the case. But mostly I was afraid the police would think I was a crackpot and a time waster, and just wouldn't believe me. I had to have faith in my skills though—I realised that—and only through contacting the police would I be able to stand by my word to Jacqui, as I had promised, and to myself and my convictions as a serious practising psychic.

What happened next was the most shocking, disturbing, profound and important thing that I have ever experienced. First, I heard her voice as if it was coming from a distance. She had taken my hand and we were suddenly somewhere else; it was now possible for Jacqui to show me every detail of what had happened to her, from the moment she opened the door of her flat to her visitor, to the moment she stood looking down at her own dead body. Her feelings of helplessness and anger consumed me.

In an instant I was no longer in the safety of my bedroom; I was in a flat somewhere, not that far away, still in Ruislip. I knew it was hers as, through her, I was completely aware of my surroundings. My body was her body. Her thoughts became my thoughts and everything became clear to me. I could hear her voice deep in my mind telling me she should have been at work that night. She had been waiting on a message from a friend and wasn't feeling very well anyway, so she had decided to stay at home. I could feel her stomach pains and discomfort as she moved around the flat. It was a small council flat and she kept it extremely neat. Everything seemed to be put away and in order, except for a prescription for some painkillers, which was lying on the coffee table. Again I heard her voice within me, explaining: 'I had intended having an early night but two visitors arrived earlier. Both of them were innocent. They were offering me a job.'

I saw images of Jacqui's flat, everything so clear it was as if I was watching television, with the images flicking before me in freeze frame shots, yet within me I could feel a tension and unease, I knew what was about to happen. I knew I had to remember everything I saw. I looked on, watching with my breath held tight in my chest. I would be a silent witness, unseen, helpless, as the horror unfolded before my eyes. Instinctively I looked around, taking in every detail of the room. I saw two cups, one of which had been washed up and left on the draining board and the other half-filled with coffee, before turning to take in the rest of the kitchen.

The evening played out in my head and through my eyes. Jacqui was having a cup of coffee and running a bath, 'hoping this would relieve the pain', I heard a voice say in my head. As I watched, Jacqui told me all about her jewellery and explained how 'it was her thing'. She adored jewellery, she told me, and was well-known for wearing as much as she could at any one time.

She told me she was drawing her bath in preparation for bed. She was thinking about the earlier job offer and how it tied in nicely with her plans for making a fresh start. I could feel her desire to put her life back on track. She was not going to remain in the past, thinking about her broken marriage. She was separated from her husband and was going to get a divorce. I could feel her determination to get over her past and start anew.

Then the doorbell rang and Jacqui turned off the taps in the bathroom. I was with her as she approached her front door. She opened the door slightly and there was a man standing before her. I could instantly feel the goose bumps rise on her skin because I was still in her mind as her memory unfolded. She didn't like this man. In what seemed like a millionth of a second, I knew he was not a friend but someone who was on the outskirts of her circle of friends. She knew him from being in the same social circles. He had even been in her flat once before, to fix her electricity because a friend had asked him to do it. He was a flirt, and Jacqui had always resisted his advances, because she was simply not attracted to him.

Somehow, all of this passed into my consciousness at once, as if I were Jacqui. I know this makes no sense but it is what happened. I became aware at that moment, as her thoughts raced, that her current boyfriend was in detention and that this man knew him and her boyfriend's father. Jacqui did not want to let him in, but he knew that she was expecting news from her boyfriend. He told her that he had been in touch with him that week and that he had a message for her. Believing him was a fatal mistake.

Reluctantly, she reached up and removed the safety chain, and at once her senses were in uproar, instinctively knowing she shouldn't have done that. Her gut feeling was working overtime as she moved into the living room. She was sending out messages to me about this man, trying to give me as much information as possible; he was 'a grease monkey', his birthday was in late April or May, which made him a Taurus, and he had certain tattoos on his arms. She was not happy that she had let him in, and felt very uneasy about the way he was looking at her, as if he wanted to devour her. She tried to keep these thoughts and feelings at bay but it was impossible. At one point he circled her. Was he trying to flirt with her again? Was he about to make a move? Was he just waiting for his chance? Jacqui moved away from him, to the bathroom, and I moved with her. Although her senses were working overtime she never expected what followed, or the suddenness of it.

He took her by surprise, grabbing her from behind. I could feel her terror because it was deep inside me too. She was terribly afraid, almost stunned into stillness, but then suddenly the feeling of fear, of being like a trapped animal in her flat with this man was overtaken by her desire to survive. She fought with all her might. He was in a terrible rage, but she tore at his hands with her nails, cutting into him in an effort to release his grip. The tussle was violent.

In the struggle the towel rail came away from the wall. He had her held, but turning quickly she lunged forward in a bid for freedom, making for the phone. He caught her, and I felt everything she did; I fought for my breath as she did, and watched in disbelief as this horrifying scene unfolded in front of my eyes, like something from a horror movie. The only difference was that this was real and not part of a film. He beat her and assaulted her in terrible ways I couldn't even begin to describe, and then proceeded to drag her along the hall and into the living room. She was still kicking and fighting, disturbing the once neat and tidy room. She tried to reach the phone again while calling constantly for someone called Terry.

There was a further, desperate struggle and the man wrenched her away from the phone. She had made her final bid for freedom, but it was useless.

She was trapped, and he moved in for the kill. Her terror was unreal now. Like an expert, his hand reached behind her, pulled the curtain cord down, and wrapped it tight around her neck. He showed no mercy and knew exactly what he was doing, choking her until the last breath had left her lips and she slumped into lifelessness.

As she slid to the floor her last thoughts were of her family, and her shock that this could happen to her. I looked on in horror. 'It was over very quickly,' I heard Jacqui say. 'What a bloody way to go.'

She was now dragged along the floor, along the hallway and into the living room, her spirit beside me still numb from what had happened. Her body was dumped there in a prone position, while this man stood to his feet and looked down upon her, cold as ice. Jacqui lay dead on the floor, and the moment her spirit left her body she was filled with a sense of hopelessness. Looking for help, in desperation, she had come through to me. Now I was witness to her death, to this gruesome murder. Her killer did not panic after he killed her. Instead, he coldly set about removing the rings from her fingers, and any other pieces of jewellery he could get his hands on. Two rings would not budge and he had to leave them on her. He had been there for about ten minutes, taking all that he could, all of her jewellery—in no rush—before he casually looked in the mirror, calmly surveyed the scene before him, and simply walked away.

The last image I recall seeing is that of Jacqui lying on the floor, lifeless, but in my mind I could hear her pleas for help. I was in absolute shock. I could not think straight. I was numb.

I don't know how long I stayed in Jacqui's mind, if that's the proper way to describe it, but finally, I looked around and found I was in my own bedroom once more. Everything looked the same, but for me it would never be the same, ever again.

The way I saw things changed that night. I did not feel bitter that I had experienced this, but I did feel a certain amount of helplessness. What I saw that night has never left, and will never leave me. It stays in my mind and feels like a shadow across it. Sometimes I can block it out, but mostly it is always with me, and because Jacqui spent so much time around me, there's a resonance and an identity that can never be erased. She brought me to her worst nightmare, and trusted me with it. The responsibility of someone, alive or dead, entrusting you with something like this, is both a compliment and a curse. And now I was to find that I was to be haunted, indefinitely, with a ghost's ghosts.

I lay on my bed, getting colder and colder. My mind raced. I had just witnessed a brutal attack and murder. I had lived through every second of that vicious assault and killing as if it was me being attacked, assaulted, murdered. I had survived, but Jacqui had not. This was not just any murder, this was now part of me, and it had to be solved.

- CHAPTER 4 -

Morning came and I was unable to move. I was shattered, physically and emotionally. I felt ill, and my face was stiff from the tears that had flowed from my eyes. Those tears were not my tears, they were Jacqui's. I could not control them, and they flowed as a sense of relief that she had reached somebody who could hear her pleas. Floods of tears rolled down my face, into my ears, down my neck and on to my pillow, and I was unable to brush them away, letting them simply dry where they landed. I kept asking myself the same questions—questions that went around and around in my head: *What can I do? Who will believe me? Who will take the word of a fledgling medium?*

My little family was beginning to make the familiar early morning sounds of getting up and starting the day, but I lay motionless. Young Canice popped his head around the open door and smiled at me.

'Are you awake yet?' he asked.

I was not able to nod at him or even give him the faintest hint of a smile, and he ran off calling for his mother to come and see what was wrong with his Aunt Chris.

I eventually managed to recover enough to get up, and I shared the shocking details of Jacqui's last visit with Mary, having kept her informed of the increase in disturbances since the previous Friday. After much talking and plenty of hot tea we reached a decision. There was a retired policeman I knew, and I thought that if I spoke to him he could help me in my dilemma. My situation could only be described as such.

How could I help this person who needed it so desperately? I could hear Jacqui's voice urging me over and over to go to the police, but how could I? With what story? It was one thing to realise the situation I was in and quite another to actually find the courage to go to the police with it. All I wanted to do was dive for cover and return to Ireland. I was happy providing a service to the people who came to me looking for comfort and guidance, because they believed in what I was doing and believed in me, but now I was being urged to go to the police, and I shuddered to think how they would react to me. I was sure they would think I was mentally disturbed or looking for attention.

The whole situation seemed unbelievable. How could I even begin to explain that I had witnessed a murder that happened several days before, in a flat a few miles away, but from within the safety of my own bedroom? How could I explain that the very person who told me about the murder was the victim? Or that I knew who the killer was, what his star sign was, and countless details about him, despite never having set eyes on him before? I just didn't know where I could begin, so I needed to talk to someone who could give me sound advice.

I spoke to my friend Len, the retired policeman. He listened to my story from start to finish, and in the end said that I had to contact the police, even though they might be sceptical. He suggested that I should contact Superintendent Tony Lundy, whom he knew. I made my mind up to telephone the police later that evening and I felt happy with my decision. For me, it was the right thing to do. I felt I had been contacted for a reason; to pass on this information, and to help a woman who had suffered a terrible fate find peace. Hopefully, I thought, that would be the beginning of the end of this horrible and disturbing situation.

Suddenly I could hear Jacqui telling me to ring the police 'Now! Right now!' I did as I was urged, and asked to speak to Lundy in relation to the Jacqueline Poole murder. I was told that he was not in, but at that very moment a detective named Tony Batters had just arrived into the station and as he was the investigating officer on the case he would speak with me. I told him that I had some information on the Jacqui Poole case but I held back the fact that I was a medium, afraid he might think I was just a crank. He arranged to come and speak to me at home, and having committed myself to Jacqui, I agreed, feeling rather scared but satisfied that I was at least fulfilling my promise to Jacqui.

I THINK MY decision would have been made even easier had I known that the poor young woman, just 25 years old, had been lying on the floor of her flat for two days before her body was found. To think that all around her people were going about their own lives, oblivious to her tortured spirit and the ghastly way in which she had been taken by a vicious attacker in what the police described as 'really a nasty murder', made me feel angry, and terribly sad. It was only when a concerned friend had not seen her for two days and tried to phone her that suspicions were aroused. The friend grew alarmed when the phone was not answered, and got in touch with the police. It was a terrible sight for the young policeman who, along with Jacqui's boyfriend's father, George Lee Senior, broke down the door of her flat and found her. Had I known the circumstances of her tragic discovery I wouldn't have hesitated for a moment.

Ruislip was a busy little suburb not far from London's city centre. It had a village feel to it and news travelled fast. But I just didn't want to hear anything about the murder that was being talked about around town. It was far too close to me because it felt like it had actually happened to me too. I had lived, and died, the experience, and nobody ever gets to come through and wake up the next day to tell the tale. Any mere mention of the attack would send shivers through my spine and fill me with the worst feelings imaginable. I just wanted to pass on the information and get it over with.

As soon as I put down the phone after speaking with the police, the questions came, and stayed with me, causing me to agonise over them. *Why me? Why did this happen to me?* I was a woman of no real importance in the grand scheme of things. I was a young woman living a quiet life in a suburb near West London, and apart from my clients, who had remained at a constant number, I doubt if many would have noticed my coming or going. So why had this young woman chosen me to help her? Was it purely because I lived nearby? Could she somehow sense that I had the ability to communicate with those passed on? Was it fate that let me to live so close to where she herself lived? It was very unlikely to find a medium so close to the scene of the murder. There wasn't any other medium in Ruislip as far as

I knew, but there were some dotted around Harrow and South Harrow, not more than 15 minutes from Ruislip. I have always been puzzled as to why Jacqui chose me. But choose me she did, and I felt compelled to ask myself, what did it mean to me?

These questions and my attempts to answer them left me in a state of confusion until finally I decided that it wasn't down to me to find out the reasons for everything. All I knew was that I could do no more than give my story, or should I say Jacqui's story, to the police, regardless of my fears.

I did still cringe inwardly, though, at the thought of my impending interview with Batters. I didn't need to be a rocket scientist to work out the reaction that awaited me. I was very sure of one thing, and that was that I would face my first real test, the first test of my credibility. Most of the people who had come to me before had been looking for answers, had believed in my abilities and my honesty, but this would be very different, and I dreaded the thoughts of facing sceptical police officers. I knew that the stories would fly about me after such an interview, and I even feared their immediate reaction. Would the police get up and leave? Or be polite enough to hear me out, then leave, laughing at me? I didn't want that, but not just for myself, but because Jacqui was relying on me. I was the only one who could help her. So here I was, a young Irish girl, living and working in England, and now I had to convince the British Police that I had witnessed a murder, and that my information came entirely from the murdered victim. How do you even begin to explain that to someone?

I was wary of their reaction, but I felt I had no choice. I had to give them a little background to ease them into what would undoubtedly be an extraordinary story, and I had to convince them I wasn't deranged. I wanted to bring things back and explain how I came to realise I had a special ability, the double-edged sword of being a medium, given a power I sometimes see as a gift, and sometimes as a curse. I feel tremendously honoured and privileged to have this ability, and find great satisfaction in being able to help and comfort those in need in a way very few can do, but there are times when I wish I hadn't seen what I have, or known what I have known, because sometimes I am left with knowledge I can do nothing about, and can only stand back and watch helplessly as terrible events unfold.

- CHAPTER 5 -

THERE WAS NO mistaking my thoughts on whether I had a gift or a curse when it came to that week in Ruislip in 1983. The sheer horror of what I had experienced through the visions and feelings of Jacqui Poole's murder, and the anxiety I felt at having to convince the police that I was telling the truth, knowing that so much was at stake—the very peace of a departed soul—left me feeling that this time, my sixth sense was definitely a terrible burden.

I had not chosen to see what I had seen, or feel what I had felt. I had not been providing a service for anybody, I did not go looking for this, and had nothing to gain from it. I did not want to go to the police, but felt compelled to by the constant and persistent pleas of the victim's spirit, urging me on.

She would not leave me alone; she was haunting me every moment.

It got to the stage where my sister Mary would wonder if I was always talking to myself. In time, I became so used to Jacqui being around that I found myself treating her as if she were alive. Even when I wasn't sure if she was in the room, I would subconsciously find myself talking to her.

I steeled myself for the police, but was still quite nervous. I think most people would be nervous if the police were coming to interview them, and in this situation that feeling was multiplied by a thousand. I was still shook from the memory of the murder, and felt that I might be laughed at for what I was about to say, but when the police arrived I knew there was no going back, and I just had to get through this.

They took a seat while I gave them a little background about myself, explaining anxiously who I was and what it was I did, in a way that wouldn't make them immediately think I was a crank.

Batters introduced himself and his partner. He was a typical detective. He kept his own counsel and trusted no one. His colleague remained distant, simply listening to what I said. His body language gave nothing away. I took no heed and slowly began to tell my story. This was too important to ruin before we even got started. I told them that I had been troubled by psychic experiences since my childhood in Ireland, giving them a few examples, and that I had experienced some more that week, after spending a very upsetting weekend phoning my friends to see if something was up with any of them.

They looked at me and then at each other with quizzical looks, and I could tell they were not going to be an easy audience. I didn't blame them for this, because I felt that my knowledge of the crime was going to be very difficult for them to digest. To ignore all their instincts, throw their training and caution to the wind, to not only listen to what I had to say but also to believe me, was going to take some work.

I told them that I wanted to describe and explain all that I could about Jacqueline Poole's murder, and try to include every single piece of information I could remember, not wanting to leave out anything in case it would become the one clue that would lead to the killer. I knew they might not believe me but I had to explain that Jacqui herself had communicated with me and told and shown me everything that had happened. I could hear myself talking to them and knew it all sounded so strange, but what else could I do?

At that moment I felt the presence of Jacqui beside me, guiding me on, encouraging me to be strong, and to tell them everything I knew about the crime. I started at the beginning. I mentioned that when Jacqui first came to me she had called herself Jacqui Hunt, not Poole. Even if this was true, which I didn't know at the time, I could sense that they did not believe me, and were only listening to me out of courtesy and a little curiosity. I suppose they might have thought I could have known her, or a member of her family. We didn't live that far apart, after all.

I could feel that Jacqui was definitely with me now in spirit, and she suggested that I should ask one of them for a personal belonging, to see if I could convince them that I was not a fraud. The other detective gave me his car keys, a little warily, not sure if he should even entertain my request in case it was seen to be encouraging me to continue with my bizarre story.

Another of my abilities is that I have long been able to psychometrise with people's belongings, having the ability to tell people personal information about themselves and their family just by touching something small that they own. I took the detective's keys in my hand and instantly received images and information about his life. I told him that he would need to get the house that he was thinking of buying rewired or he would not get the mortgage. He glanced at me with a curious look, trying not to betray his puzzlement at how I knew he was thinking of buying a house. He looked at Batters then, in a strange way, as if confirming that what I said was true. I also told him that he would be transferred to another station very soon, and then to really make sure I had convinced them, I told him something of a personal and very private nature. I will never divulge the nature of this personal message that was for him and his colleague only, but I think I managed to convince them that I was not a fraud or a crank, and that I did indeed have an ability that might come in useful. The information I gave them was so private that it would have been impossible for me to have known it without having some sort of ability beyond the norm. Their scepticism wavered, and together, they looked willing to give this unusual approach some time, to hear me out. If all else failed, they could at least give it a try and see if I could point them in the right direction.

When they came to interview me, the police were in the process of interviewing countless numbers of people and had taken statements from over a thousand witnesses, taking on an exhaustive door-to-door enquiry process, but I didn't know how successful their investigation had been. I could only hope that my own evidence would back up what they already knew, somehow provide the final piece of the puzzle to catch the killer and bring him to justice.

I didn't want to just relive the whole dreadful experience again, because I was afraid the police might think it was a bit too much, and too dramatic to be real. It wasn't just about telling them what had happened; this was about providing them with all the information they needed to catch the killer, and I was willing to let Jacqui guide me through the details in the way she thought best.

Having caught their attention with my accuracy when psycometrising, I explained that I would now reveal the details of the attack, the murder location, the killer, everything I could, by going into a trance and letting Jacqui's words come through me. I took a breath, closed my eyes, felt them flutter open and then closed them again, and with Jacqui's spirit guiding me, I began my description of the scene and the terrible event, mentioning everything in minute detail, just as I had seen it.

The two policemen leaned forward in their chairs, waiting to hear my story, or as it was, Jacqui's story, through me. Batters looked sceptical. They would never have heard evidence from the victim of a murder before, but despite my history as a medium and psychic, this was completely new to me too, and I wasn't sure what was going to come of it. It was only Jacqui's pleading voice asking me to go on that gave me the determination to continue, to try to give her the peace she needed and to give her killer the justice she deserved.

- CHAPTER 6 -

THE INFORMATION CAME in fits and starts as Jacqui guided me through her terrible story.

'She shouldn't have been there,' I said.

'She was supposed to be going to work ... two men came for her earlier but she didn't want to go ... she wasn't feeling well.' I heard myself repeat the words: 'She wasn't supposed to be there.'

I went on to describe how Jacqui was showing me the chain on the door, describing how she wasn't sure about letting in this man who had just called, but that she thought he had a message from her boyfriend.

'That's why she let him in,' I explained.
I told them how Jacqui knew the man socially, as a friend of a friend rather than as a close friend or ex-boyfriend. 'Part of a group of friends,' I suddenly heard myself say. I explained how she never liked

this bloke who was becoming a bit of a pest, visiting her at work in the local grocers or at the bar where she served as a barmaid. She had made it clear she wasn't interested, and had told him she would tell someone else about his persistent flirting with her if he didn't stop. I got a sense that the police wanted to know how she had met this man in the first place.

'The link is with the nick. Both had the same friend who was in the nick,' Jacqui told me to say, and I explained that that was where her boyfriend, George Lee was.

I said that Jacqui was now talking about robbery and showing me some jewellery; a St. Christopher medal, a chunky bracelet, and mentioned that not everything was taken, that some rings had been left behind. The detectives looked at each other, and then went back to taking down the details. *Was I giving them what they wanted? Was the information helping them at all? Did it confirm what they already knew?* I had no idea, but I had to continue.

I was being prompted by Jacqui to give more information about her, to give a background, so I said that Jacqui had suffered from depression, and was taking pills for it. She still had a prescription, which was on the table. I told them how she was going through a divorce, and was thinking about her husband, but was also looking forward to getting on with her life and moving on. I explained how she wanted to keep her personal life quiet because she was around the wrong people in the past, and was trying to start afresh.

I told them that Jacqui told me that she worked in three bars around the Hillingdon area, but that she had been drinking more than she should. Meanwhile, she kept asking for Terry, and with that other names came to mind, but I wasn't sure of the order she wanted me to mention them in, and I didn't know if they would mean anything to the police, who would surely already have contacted family and friends, and made a list of everyone she knew.

The names Betty, Sylvia, and Gloria came to me then. The two policemen took down the names, every now and then exchanging curious glances. Terry, I felt, was Jacqui's eldest brother, and was very close to her. I suddenly got the name Barbara Stone, but I wasn't sure from where. I felt I was getting confused, so I moved on to something else.

'Now she's showing me where she lives,' I said, but I was still confused, and the details weren't coming through as clearly as they normally would. All I could say was that there were two lots of flats; that the road started with the letter L; and there was a car park.

'He parked on the corner ... there's a car park,' I suddenly realised. I told them he had been there before and had done a job for Jacqui in the past.

Jacqui urged me to move on to the details I definitely knew, because she had shown me herself, and I had experienced the horror of the murder scene as if I had been standing there. I gave a clear description of how I had seen the victims' flat at first, and how the furniture was arranged.

'There's a hallway, with a newspaper. It's not read. And there's a cupboard. There are two cups in the kitchen. One is washed up ... there's just two cups. She had made a cup of coffee.'

Batters, who looked really sceptical throughout my opening speech, immediately became more interested, as he had been the first officer at the scene of the murder. I could tell that he was becoming convinced, that my descriptions were accurately matching what he had seen when he first entered the scene of the crime.

Maybe they were becoming a little unsettled by how close I was to the facts. Maybe they were thinking at this stage that I must have heard or been told the finer points of the case, somehow. After all, that would be the more rational explanation. They asked me several questions to see if there was any way I could have obtained my information elsewhere, any way I could have known. Jacqui had been murdered a couple of days before I'd heard anything from anyone about it, and even then it was only a conversation overheard in the village, nothing more. I was feeling so drained, so dreadful that I tried to ignore the story and just didn't want to believe that what was happening to me was related. I understood the police asking me these questions though. They had to be thorough, and look for likely, reasonable explanations.

For 30 minutes they asked me about possible sources for what I knew, from somehow knowing Jacqui's family and friends, to knowing police who had been at the scene. As an Irish girl living in a quiet part of Ruislip, I had no real way of knowing either. They then asked a lot of questions about my personal life and my written notes. When they were satisfied that I had absolutely no connection with the victim's family, and that I had no contact with any police or anybody else who might know something about the case, they returned to the investigation.

Again, I wondered how I could possibly convince them that instead of having a connection to Jacqui's family, I had a most intense spiritual connection to Jacqui herself, who at that very moment was guiding my answers and giving the detectives the information they needed. Whether they believed me or not, they were writing down absolutely everything I was saying, and this was a promising sign to me.

I went on telling them what Jacqui was showing me, explaining that she kept drawing me into the bathroom, then into the living room.

'She couldn't get to the phone,' I said. I tried to describe everything in detail as much as I could, in part to help the police investigation, but also to try to convince them I was telling the truth about Jacqui being there with me and speaking through me.

'There was an envelope and letter. It had just come. There's a black address book. The room is small and nice, but you found it in a different state. The furniture was rearranged, the settee cushions were moved out of place.'

I clearly recall that Batters looked shocked but enthralled when I said these words. I would find out later that my descriptions were completely accurate and without any error matched the flat's appearance and layout when he had first arrived on the murder scene. I went on to describe Jacqui herself, telling them she was wearing jeans and a jumper. 'I changed my clothes twice,' she told me.

The tone changed as I went on to describe the brutal attack on Jacqui, and I could feel her getting angrier and angrier as she recalled the horrible event. I gave a huge amount of personal details about how she died, which she told me herself, that remain to this day strictly confidential, found only on police files. Batters and his colleague just looked at me in amazement as I described the horrible things that had been done and the damage that had been inflicted before the killer decided he had had enough and decided to take her life. They had seen the pathologist's report and knew every single thing I said was true, and unnervingly accurate. At that moment I knew they believed me. There was simply no other way I could have known in such minute detail what had happened to Jacqui. There was still a long way to go though.

There was such an air of deep sadness and anger coming from Jacqui's spirit now. She had sworn over and over when describing the attack, and had not let up, until with a resigned sigh I finally said, repeating what Jacqui had told me, 'It's over very quickly ... what a bloody way to go. She's being dragged along the floor. Along the hallway.'

I felt an awful feeling inside me like nothing I could ever describe. I was having trouble going on. I had to stop. I felt my eyelids flutter rapidly, and after a few seconds I returned to a normal state, no longer tied to Jacqui's spirit, but exhausted and distressed, no longer reliving the awful scene but sitting safely in my own quiet house.

'I'm sorry, I had to stop,' I said.

The policemen looked concerned. I got the feeling they were completely enthralled.

'How are you feeling?'

'Very tired. It takes it out of you.'

'Will you be able to carry on?'

I wasn't sure. To be honest, I wasn't even sure what I had told them. It was as if Jacqui had taken over while my own consciousness took a back seat and just switched off.

'What do you need to know?' I asked. 'I don't know where we're at. Was it helpful?'

'Extremely interesting. But we need more on the murderer. Is there more?'

I said I'd try again in a few minutes, after I had recovered my breath.

☙ ☙ ☙ ☙ ☙

We had some coffee, during which time the detectives quizzed me again on any possible sources I may have had, but there was simply no way I could have known what I did in such detail unless I had been in contact with the victim somehow. I think they knew I wasn't lying. What they didn't know, I guess, was how I had been in contact with the victim when the victim was dead.

'Can you get a name from what I've given you?' I asked. They shook their heads.

'I have not been able to understand what she calls him,' I told them.

It was bothering me that I couldn't understand and give the police the one thing that would be the most important of all: the name of the murderer. I was determined to get to the bottom of it and so I said I would try again after a short break. After a while I was ready to start again, and only a few seconds later I was able to tune into Jacqui's spirit once more. They asked me for a description of what the murderer looked like and with the help of Jacqui, describing and explaining everything in whispered words, I told them that he was about 5'8, not much more, had dark skin and had wavy Afro-style hair. Some of the details became unclear as Jacqui's spirit grew angry or dismayed, but I tried my best to stay focused and give an accurate description.

'Jacqui is sending me pictures of him,' I said.

'He is in his early twenties and Jacqui knows him, but he is not a friend. His birthday is in late April or May, his star sign is Taurus. He has tattoos on his arms, a sword, a snake, a rose? He's been working lately on painting or decorating, but he doesn't have a regular job. He's got into places before. He's clever with cars. I get a name: Tony, but he has a nickname, not a real name ... I still can't understand what she is saying to me.'

If they could get that they might really be on to something. If this turned out to be correct, of course. I had heard Jacqui tell me over and over what this nickname was, but it hadn't made any sense to me. I wasn't sure if her voice wasn't coming through properly because of her anger, or because of some other interference, whether I was too tired to hear her properly, or if I just didn't understand the word she was saying. I retained my Irish accent and at times a localised English accent could give me trouble with the odd word here and there. I carried on anyway, and said that the man was local, and that he had spoken to the police already. This got them very interested again. A man called Tony they had already spoken to? That would seriously narrow things down, and could even lead them straight to the killer.

I went on: 'The guy lives on an estate, in a council flat. He likes to drink. He's still around, drinking with friends. He was drinking with friends the night before all of this. He's got a girlfriend who knows Jacqui. She's dark haired, small and pretty.'

Again the details became unclear and all I could get was that her name had the initial C in it. Then a message from Jacqui came through very clearly indeed:

'You have the right group. You are close.' This was directed straight at the police, followed by the advice: 'Look at his alibi.'

I explained further that the killer had simply walked away from the murder scene, and didn't seem to show any emotion at all.

Jacqui gave me more information then, telling me something about an insurance claim, and bringing up the name Sylvia again. Then Betty was mentioned. Something about her mother's friend? It was so confusing. There was something about her mother, and something about a friend living over a newspaper shop, and Jacqui hinted at finding more information from these sources. All of this was helping, I felt, but there was still one major thing that needed to be discovered—the killer's name. I still couldn't understand what Jacqui was trying to tell me, and I sensed her getting angrier every time she even thought about him, while I was getting distracted because I was getting more and more frustrated, so I needed to do something different. A new approach was needed.

'I know you want his name,' I said to the police. 'I couldn't get it. She's not making sense. I can try to write it.'

They looked puzzled. 'How will you write it if you can't understand it?'

I took a pen and some paper, and told them I would simply be holding the pen, and that Jacqui would be writing the name of her killer. The policemen looked both surprised and confused, so I explained that I would try to go into a trance again, and ask Jacqui to write down the name of her killer, through me. I felt Jacqui also wanted to tell us where her jewellery had been hidden by her killer. I would have to let her take over.

I think they thought I was mad, sitting there asking out loud for the help of the girl who had been murdered. They just did not realise how much she was around us as we sat in my living room that day, or at that stage that she was in my mind constantly prompting me as to what to say to the officers.

Sitting in an armchair with an open notebook on my lap, I relaxed and went into a trance, feeling Jacqui's spirit enter my body, before everything went dark for me. Though I did not have control of my body or mind, I was aware enough to know that after about 30 seconds the pen began to shake, scribbling in one area of the paper. It then moved to another part of the sheet, and wrote one word very slowly and jerkily. The pen then moved to another point, started to write, but then stopped. It started again after a few seconds, and wrote a word. I couldn't see what my hand was doing as my eyes were closed, and I definitely had no control over it, or the pen that was now scribbling away. A few minutes later, I felt my own consciousness return and looked down at the paper with the two

officers to see what had been written. I was as eager
to know as they were.

Batters seemed to go a little pale, as if a shiver
had just gone down his spine. The name on the pad
was clear: 'Pokie'.

I wasn't to know, but at that moment, Batters knew
who had killed Jacqui Poole. The words 'Ikeham'
and 'garden', and the number 221 were also written
on the pad. I presumed this was a possible hiding
place for the jewellery, and the police presumed it
was a mis-spelling of nearby Ickenham. With the
name, I felt there was more to tell, and stressed
that the police should collect any clothes that this
'Pokie' might be getting rid of. I repeated this to
them, because I somehow knew that it would be
of vital importance. I also felt prompted to remind
them that he would have a good alibi and that none
of his friends would believe he could be capable of
murder.

They did seem very interested in what I had
said. A man called Tony Ruark, with the nickname
'Pokie' had spoken to them after the murder, but
had seemed quite calm and collected. Looking back
at that moment, I guess the detectives thought they
might have their man. They just had to prove it.

❖ ❖ ❖ ❖ ❖

WE FINISHED UP after that; the detectives grateful
but still very much confused and intrigued by what
had taken place, not quite sure what they had just

witnessed and even more unsure how exactly to report back what they had been told, and how it had been discovered.

There wasn't much more that I could do. I had come forward as Jacqui had asked me, and had given all the information I could to the police. I hoped that would be the end of my part in this terrible and tragic event, and that my own life would start to return to normal, unburdened by that awful feeling of gloom and despair that had surrounded me since Jacqui had first tried to contact me. I hoped the police would find her killer so that she could finally rest in peace and that justice would be served. I could only hope the police had taken me seriously enough to double-check everything I had told them. I had a very strong feeling that I had got everything right and had stressed the importance of retaining any clothes this 'Pokie' character may have tried to throw out. I didn't know if it would help, but I felt this would be an important clue in the case.

After the detectives left they reported back to Detective Superintendent Tony Lundy, who advised them to interview me again. I didn't know what else I could tell them, and felt dismayed. However, I was pleased to hear that after my interviews, the police had become suspicious enough of 'Pokie' Ruark to completely re-check his movements. Following concerns which then arose around his alibi, he was arrested. Officers then dug up two gardens; Jacqui's and another next to the flats where Ruark lived, but nothing was found. They did recover an old pullover Ruark had thrown into a waste bin due for collection, but there was no hard evidence linking him to the murder.

I was relieved in a way that my part was over. I had done all I could and now it was the turn of the police to do their job. I just wanted it all to end. The brutal murder of that poor woman had affected me deeply, in a way nothing before or since would ever match, and now more than ever I was unsettled by my psychic abilities. I just wanted to forget about Jacqui Poole's murder, and move on. However this was going to prove much harder than I could have ever imagined.

- CHAPTER 7 -

THE MURDER AND the emotional turmoil inflicted upon me as a result of being Jacqui's medium was synonymous with the route my gift had been taking over the years, showing me progressively darker things and coming to a head in Ruislip. There was a time when my gift provided me with comfort and curiosity, and was something I shared with people easily. Now it was a burden, and I wished it would go away.

Those first few years away from home, when I had escaped from the confines of Stradbally and worked on the Isle of Man and then in the UK were the happiest of my life, and visions just didn't affect me. When I had gone to the Isle of Man I tried to banish all thoughts of psychic powers and instead used all my mental energies to focus on that most important of subjects for a 15-year-old girl: boys!

Unfortunately, there were some exceptions, and some incidents when my ability began to intrude on my happiness. Word got out that I was able to read tea leaves and that was that. I reluctantly read the leaves for my friend Pat, a girl from Scotland, and the only thing I could see was the death of a woman. One hour later we received a phone call informing Pat that her boyfriend's mother had just died. I was stunned, and so was Pat, and I didn't read another tea leaf while I was there.

I moved on to Highcroft in Surrey then. It was the late 60s and I was excited to be in England to seek my fortune. That fortune never materialised but I did have my sister Mary already there waiting for me. I found work easily enough in a hotel catering for retired and old, upper class people, and naturally enough it was haunted.

It wasn't long after I started working there that I began seeing things again. One morning I woke up with sleep in my eyes to the sight of a woman in my room. I presumed it was the owner, Miss Pickles, come to wake me up. She smiled and then went away. I tried to catch 40 winks but just as I was dozing off I was interrupted by Miss Pickles, walking into the room again. I jumped up immediately and told her I was sorry to have her come in to me again. She didn't know what I was talking about.

She asked, 'What do you mean? This is the first time I have been up to you,' and as the other girls started to get up, they wondered what I was talking about. I muttered that the place must be haunted, not really thinking much of it. The other girls were up and out of their rooms quick enough, however. It gradually dawned on me that the person I had seen was a woman my mother had worked for back in Stradbally, who had passed over a few years before. I smiled when I recalled telling her husband about the man I saw regularly in his hallway. He had just smiled and said, 'Those who are gone before us will never harm you.' I found great comfort in that, but all that day I kept getting strange looks, and after that incident I got used to hearing strange noises.

My childhood friend Joe returned to me and I often heard him calling me. One night, when I was sitting on a set of swings in the local park with my sister Mary, I felt Joe's presence and I sensed a warning. I jumped off the swing immediately and insisted that we should return to the hotel. The very next day we heard that the police were looking for a man who had attacked a woman in that area that very night. I was very grateful for Joe's warning, and at times like that I knew my sixth sense could be a blessing.

Next morning I went into the dining room as usually to check that everything was in order before the guests came down for breakfast. I noticed that the salt-cellars on my tables had been emptied all over the place. I had some job to clean up the mess. The next day it happened again. This continued for a time with no explanation, until one morning, clearer than ever, I heard Joe's voice calling me.

He called out my name and I followed his voice out to the garden. It was a large garden with many beautiful trees and as I walked I heard him calling me. On my return to the dining room I glanced at the floor and saw a brooch. I picked it up and gave it to Miss Pickles. Later that day one of the guests came to thank me. She had lost her mother's brooch while out walking and was more than surprised when I had found it, because she had given up all hope of ever doing so. I could not tell her that a ghost had helped me, but I was glad of the praise anyway.

That place was definitely one of the most haunted places I have ever been in. One night I had been out with my sister Mary and came home a bit late. I was no good when it came to drink but I had taken a glass of wine and felt a little tipsy as a result. Mary had gone up to bed ahead of me and I did not delay too long after her as the place was really creepy. As I went upstairs I said goodnight to Lady Jane, one of the guests, and then a few other people who all seemed to be walking up or down the stairs. It didn't dawn on me that it was strange that there was such traffic on the stairs at that hour of the night. The next day Lady Jane asked me if I had been walking or talking in my sleep as I had been saying goodnight to quite a few people on the stairs that night, but when I described to her the people I had bid goodnight, she went very pale and realised that I had surely seen something and had not been talking to myself.

There were several other nights when the door to the bar opened and closed and glasses seemed to be left on tables, but myself and Mary decided to keep it to ourselves as the place was short staffed enough without scaring off those who were left.

I moved on to a nursing home in Hampshire after that but there was no escape from the visions and premonitions I was now having on a regular basis. I awoke one night to the sight of a priest standing over my bed. He was holding either a Bible or a prayer book in his hand, and told me that my prayers were needed for some souls who had died that night. I really didn't want these disturbing visions to intrude on my life anymore, but filled with worry, I said a few prayers before falling into a restless, haunted sleep. My dreams were filled with fire, and everywhere people were running, screaming with terror. Terrible nightmares stayed with me for the night and when I woke up in the morning I was really upset, but even more so because I couldn't tell anyone about it. I was sick of being seen as a bit strange.

Over breakfast, my new boss's husband told me about a fire in Dublin and the minute he started to tell me the details the blood drained from my face. He thought I must have had relatives there because of my reaction, which I didn't, but he wasn't to know that I was distraught because I had dreamt about it the night before. I had seen the terrifying scenes first-hand. This was the tragic disaster at the Stardust nightclub, when a Valentine's Night Ball had ended in disaster after a fire broke out and 48 young lives were lost. The Stardust tragedy left a serious mark on the lives of so many that even today you only have to mention the words and people instantly remember it. Investigations into what happened are still ongoing.

I really wasn't keen to have foreseen this scene, as at the time I had started to enjoy a normal life, going out and socialising, meeting young men and starting friendships. But as I had feared, it started off a whole series of visitations and premonitions that I couldn't ignore. I guess I was just supposed to accept them and try to get on with my own life. But this premonition irked me to the very core. My age-old childhood fear of fires came back to haunt me, my belief in God made me feel that my prayers were needed, and my gut feeling that this was the start of some more things to come turned my stomach into knots and then into stone. But I was angry—what good are prayers if they don't actually save anyone? What good is my ability if I can't save anyone? What use am I, or am I simply to live everyone else's lessons with them, in sympathy for them? This theme was to become a relentless mantra with me, constantly questioning the reasons for my premonitions and it was very tiring, frustrating and depressing.

At this point I was really starting to see it as a misguided talent rather than a helpful force. A young man I was seeing left me a note saying he was going away, never to return. This same young man came to me one night as a spirit, thanking me for our time together. I later found out that he had died of cancer. He had never told me. It was frustrating to me that I couldn't use my ability to know these things before they happened.

Looking back now I realise that this happened exactly as it should have. If I could have used my ability to change the course of events then that would not have been normal. Being with this man and letting him make his own decisions and being affected by them was one of the more normal things that happened to me, and for that, I am glad my ability was closed off from his illness. Maybe because he was so resolute about how he was going to handle everything made it impossible for me to pick up on anything. Maybe he wasn't a distressed soul that needed guiding or help or compassion. Maybe he and I were exactly how we were supposed to be, and that I can live with.

I moved to London to join my sister and after a struggle to find somewhere to live—at this time it was very hard for Irish people to find a place in London—we eventually managed to move into a cramped flat owned by a lovely couple from Guyana. I became friendly with their niece, who persuaded me to read her tea leaves for her. I was wary of getting back into this, but I couldn't turn her down after the kindness her relatives had shown me, and I saw it as a one-off. But soon I was reading for her family and friends and it became a regular session.

It was giving me a few bob to help me survive until I found a job, so I got back into it.

True to form, the visions and ghosts started to appear again with more frequency. I was surprised but happy to hear that some friends saw them too. It was great not to be alone, the only strange one. I remember walking into a friend's house and seeing an old woman standing at the top of the stairs, her arms folded, staring down at me. I was frozen to the spot, and when I cautiously mentioned it to my friend, she replied, with full nonchalance:

'Well I'm glad you met my friend. She's there a while. Wait till you meet my other friend.'

I couldn't believe it; here I was in the middle of spirits again. I got to meet her 'other friend' soon enough. He was a gentleman, but the lady didn't like him being there and when he invaded her space we would know all about it, with doors and windows opening and closing and lights going on and off. The lady felt she was there first so she had rights to the house, and that this man was getting in her way, and she wasn't at all shy about letting us know. It was really quite interesting to see. For me this was fine, to see spirits around me, with no harm done to anything, but it was a different story when I was haunted by terrifying visions and premonitions that I knew I could do nothing about, and I dreaded their return, which I knew was inevitable. I wasn't wrong.

On 27 August 1979 I had a really big premonition and I knew it would be not the last. I was in my kitchen and I could suddenly see an image of pieces of a boat floating in water, and then a royal crest. I didn't know what it was all about, but it filled me with a physical revulsion. I knew something terrible had happened. The remains of the boat were spread out over a wide area of water with all the personal bits and pieces floating about like flotsam and jetsam. I felt ill seeing these images in my mind, with no knowledge of what boat it was, where it was, or why it had happened. All I had to go on was the image of the royal crest that flashed across my mind. I had a strange feeling that this was one of three things, all connected, that would happen that day.

I found out later that day that Lord Louis Mountbatten, the Queen's cousin, had been murdered by the IRA at Donegal Bay in Sligo, when they blew up his boat. I didn't even know that Mountbatten went to Ireland on holiday. Prince Philip had also survived a bomb attack in Brussels, and horrifically, 18 British soldiers were killed by the IRA at Warrenpoint, County Down. I had seen flashes of this horrible scene of carnage as two bombs took the lives of so many young men, leaving a trail of desolation.

I hated, and still hate, getting these premonitions when I knew that it was impossible for me to prevent anything from happening. Nobody in their right mind welcomes these visions and premonitions. These are the bad times when I just feel totally helpless and think that I am cursed. That is strong language to use, but when images of tragedy, suffering, death, and pain infringe on my day to day life and I am not in a position to prevent the things I see from happening, or even prevent seeing the visions themselves; that is when I consider my gift a curse. I can think of no other word to define it.

It was around this time that I sensed I needed to go home, and spent a lot of time with my cousin Kathleen. Her story really only strengthened my belief at this time that second sight was not always to be seen as a gift, and could at times be truly, truly awful.

When I think of Kathleen nowadays I smile a happy, contented smile, because of the long years of friendship we shared. She was like a sister to me. We had a special bond because of her own sixth sense, which brought us closer. We used to go out to our favourite pub, which was only open once a week, preparing to close down, and have a great laugh, catching up on old times. We went to the pub together on my last night home, and because she was drinking, she wouldn't drive. As she left, I made her promise me she wouldn't hitch a lift on the way. She promised she would wait for the bus. Earlier that day I had read her tea leaves, and I had seen an accident and an ambulance. I stressed again that she was not to hitch, no matter what, and she repeated her promise. That was the last conversation I had with her. I remember leaving the pub worried, hoping to God I would see her again soon.

I went back to England the next day and tried to get back into the swing of things over there. That night, I suddenly saw a vision of a coffin in our local church in Stradbally, surrounded by lots of flowers. I instantly felt overwhelmingly sad, and tears started to flow from my eyes. I couldn't understand what the vision was telling me. All I could remember feeling was a grim certainty that one of my family members, or someone close to the family, was going to die. I don't have to explain how horrible a feeling that is. I thought that maybe it was to do with my friend's mother, who had been quite ill for some time.

The next night I was woken by a very bad dream. I had seen Kathleen, and she was injured or hurt in some way. It upset me so much that I couldn't think straight and was really upset and very unhappy. My weekend was really unsettled anyway, because I was thinking constantly of my friend's mother. It was her time; I could sense it, and felt sure it was she who was passing over to the other side.

But when I received a letter on Tuesday morning I was shocked to the core. I couldn't believe what I was reading: Kathleen had died two days earlier. She had been involved in an accident on the Saturday night, the very night I had seen her. I was devastated and heartbroken. I didn't know about the funeral, which obviously I would have gone to, until it was all over. Despite her promise, she had hitched a lift on the way home that night and was involved in a fatal car crash. I was devastated at the news, but more so because I seemed to already know it was going to happen and again, there was nothing I could do to stop it. I had told her not to hitch, had repeated it, and made her promise, but then I don't think anybody would really believe 100% the reasons why if I were to give them, even Kathleen, who knew all about sixth sense. Her own prediction that somebody was going to get killed on the stretch of road she hated had come true, but she wasn't to know that she would be that someone.

I cannot for the life of me remember why I received a letter about Kathleen's death, and not a phone call. I can only assume it was because my mother and father didn't have a phone at that stage. All the same, the way in which I heard, and the unsettling dreams beforehand, had once again left me feeling irked, disconnected and feeling passionately alone.

- CHAPTER 8 -

IT WAS SHORTLY after that that things started going bump in the night again. I was very sad, of course, but a couple of nights after Kathleen's death things started happening that at times gave me comfort and at other times gave me cause for concern. First of all the light in my bedroom started flashing on and off, and I suspected it was Kathleen trying to get in touch with me. I thought I heard the sound of somebody calling me in distress, and it worried me greatly. As I dropped off to sleep I heard my name being called again. I woke up and standing at the very end of my bed was Kathleen, just like I always remembered her; the cigarette in one hand and her bag under her arm. She had a little jacket on her, her trousers and her best top, and she looked very well. She was looking at me and I said to her, 'You have gone over to the other side'. She was worried about her family, she told me. Kathleen explained how she felt and how hard it was for her to accept that she had passed over. She said that they had been going along in the car, just chatting away, when all of a sudden the lights of another car came straight at them on the wrong side of the road. The driver of Kathleen's car was not drinking; he was a decent family man. There were at least 13 children left without parents that night, as the two men had quite a few children between them, and Kathleen had two little girls. It was just an awful tragedy.

For quite some time Kathleen used to come and talk to me. A few times I woke up in the middle of the night and I could just see her floating above my bed. She would be concerned about the young ones and particularly her mother, as she wasn't always well.

When Kathleen came to visit me, she simply came in. I got used to her coming in and sitting at the end of my bed, or if she was concerned about anything she would come in and tell me things and talk to me, so for quite a number of years Kathleen came through to me and explained things to me as if she was still around. She was to come to me a few years later very strongly. At the time I didn't understand why. Now, of course, I do. It was a couple of weeks before my brother committed suicide in 1986. She came to me very distressed and worried, trying to tell me something, but I didn't quite understand. I obviously didn't pick her up right or I didn't really understand the message

I was receiving. I sensed that she wanted me to go home to Ireland and often to this day I regret it, not just packing up and throwing a few things into a suitcase and going home for a few days. If I had gone at that time I would have been home, but as always 'if only' can never turn back the clock. Like Kathleen, and like anybody, I didn't really follow the advice of this sixth sense. I had seen his death in my dreams many years before, but had chosen to ignore it. I was too young then to face up to such an awful scenario, so I had chosen to pretend it didn't happen, or wasn't going to happen.

- CHAPTER 9 -

IMMEDIATELY AFTER THE murder of Jacqui Poole, the police had made an appeal to anybody who knew her to come forward and help with their enquiries. 'Pokie' Ruark did so, and claimed he was travelling by train from the Windmill Pub in Ruislip, where he had been drinking with friends, to his home four miles away at the crucial time.

I later learned that after I had named 'Pokie' Ruark to the police, his alibi was tested thoroughly, and his arrest came about because his story seemed full of holes. A customer at the Windmill saw him with a crash helmet on the evening of the murder. In custody, Ruark admitted he was using a motorbike that evening. He was a disqualified driver, resulting from vehicle theft offences, which he explained was his reason for lying. He wasn't supposed to be on the roads. There was then a 30 minute window in what had been a solid alibi beforehand. To account for the extra 30 minutes he would have had by riding a motorbike instead of getting the train, he claimed he 'ran out of petrol, and had to push it.' This could not be disproved, but the garage he named had no record of issuing a small amount of petrol and the cashier denied any transaction for a motor cycle. Ruark was an inveterate liar, and could have been engaged in crime elsewhere at the time. Everybody he had been in contact with that night was interviewed again, but there were no eye-witnesses to connect him with the actual murder, no jewellery was found at his flat, and forensic evidence was not yet advanced enough, DNA testing was not yet introduced into investigations. What complicated things further was that there were numerous other suspects interviewed who also had uncorroborated alibis.

The police knew it was Ruark who had committed the murder. Batters said as much; that after seeing Ruark's name written on the pad he instinctively knew he had 'got his man'. They just couldn't prove it. It must have been very frustrating for them to know that this man, who had obviously lied to them, was the man they were after, and to have had my information as unusable evidence (inadmissible because a ghost can't testify in court), and to be able to do nothing about it. I had given them a detailed account of Jacqui's murder, and a veritable portrait of the culprit, but none of this could be used.

Detective Batters kept every note he had written during and after his interview with me, because he was sure that one day justice would be done. But it was absolute agony for me. I couldn't even talk about the investigation, or share what I had seen with anybody, in case it might prejudice or influence things in any way. This was really hard because the murder had by now become major news in the area and was covered by all of the local and national papers. Everybody was talking about it.

I stood by for 15 months, followed, tortured, by the angry spirit of Jacqui, pleading with me to help her bring her killer to justice, but I just couldn't see what else I could do. I shared Jacqui's despair as the police were forced to admit defeat and accept that this was one crime they could not solve. They knew everything about the killer; how he did it, when, and where, but my evidence as a psychic was not admissible in court, and they knew they hadn't the means to find anything else to back up their claims. That was it for them; the investigation was wrapped up with no conclusion. But for me, and for the victim, this wouldn't be over until 'Pokie' Ruark was behind bars, and Jacqui was prepared to keep reminding me of this for as long as it took.

JACQUI CAME TO me for years after I had made my statement to the police. I feel it was her anger that kept her going, because there was no rest for her on the other side until she received justice. My life had been taken over by these events in my search for justice for Jacqui. It was hard to try and put my life back on track after all I had been through. The entire event left me burnt out and, quite honestly, depressed. I had suffered a hugely traumatic experience that—it is safe to say—very few people had ever endured and survived, and I woke up the next day as if it hadn't happened. I had been inside the mind of a woman who had been viciously attacked and murdered, had heard her pleas for help and her cries of agony, but they hadn't stopped when she had died. They had kept going, haunting and torturing me, pleading with me to do something it was not in my power to do. I was dismayed, having had far too many experiences of seeing something happen, but knowing I could do nothing to stop it. This was the worst experience yet, and it made me feel completely sick of the ability I had to see beyond the norm. I wished I never had this extra sense, and I wished that this had never happened to me. But it had, and I was trying desperately to get over it.

I have to say that whatever may be said in public about relations between the police and mediums, I received only the height of respect from the investigating officers. I know from speaking to Batters many years later, that as I was giving him my information, a lot of it came out disjointed, with a lot of the information repeated several times and perhaps not in chronological order. It is a testament to him as a policeman that he studied my statement, the most unusual statement that he ever took, and matched it in detail to the state of Jacqui's flat when he arrived as the first officer on the scene.

♣ ♣ ♣ ♣ ♣

With the passing of time and no suspect behind bars, I felt that I had let Jacqui down. I had tried so hard to help her. I had to overcome my fear of ridicule and rejection before I even approached the police with my information. I may be psychic but I am not a fool. I was fully aware what the possible reactions of the police might be. I was 100% convinced that Jacqui had come through to me across that great divide in her struggle for justice. She had fought valiantly for her life and in death her struggle continued.

For me it was a complete let down when Ruark was arrested and then let go. All that was in me raged against him for what he had done to Jacqui, and in a way, for what he had done to me. It was impossible for me to block out those dreadful images. They still haunt me. It wasn't only Jacqui constantly coming to me that upset me. There are two sides to a coin, and the opposite side to Jacqui Poole was Tony Ruark. The fact that I knew all there was to know about him ensured that I lived my life in constant fear of him. I never spoke to anyone outside of my family about him, and I could only hope that he never heard my name in conversation. I lived with the fear that he might somehow find out about me and discover where I lived. I feared for my family too, because I knew all too well Ruark's approach to life and death, and his cold indifference. If he ever found out about my knowledge of him and failed attempt to put him behind bars, then I thought my life was worthless. In all of this, I never really doubted the police and the good work they do, but fear has a way of finding a place in your brain and tearing away at it until finally it takes over. After a while, two people had laid claim to a part of my mind: Jacqui Poole and Tony Ruark.

It was a time that I would rather not remember, as I tried to pick up the pieces and move on once more with my life. Life goes on no matter how hard we try to slow the pace to suit our emotional state of mind and body. I continued with my readings, although I have to say that I was quite honestly plagued by Jacqui's interruptions. She began to visit me so often that it was driving me mad. She was bitterly disappointed, and really, really angry, which is why I did not mind as much as I could have, as I understood her frustrations. I began to see her as a friend in desperate need of help. She seemed to be a very likeable woman, someone I might have been good friends with had circumstances been different. I was touched by the similarities in our lives. We were both young women making a fresh start, but beyond that there were some striking similarities.

Jacqui, like myself, was very family orientated and was, as her sister-in-law would describe her, 'brilliant with her nieces and nephews'. This made me think of my own nephew Canice and the love and devotion I showered on him as he grew up. I was surprised to hear that Jacqui was also an animal lover, and like me when I was younger, actually had a habit of going out the back of her flat to the nearby field to feed a donkey once a week. This may seem a trivial fact but it was exactly what I used to do every Friday when I was growing up. But whereas I had my whole life ahead of me, she had hers taken away from her in a cold and vicious way, and she was furious, and kept saying to me: 'That bastard's got away with it.'

I CAME TO realise that life would never be the same for me after Jacqui. I hoped that time would heal everything but I did not know what fate held in store for me, and even though I was psychic, I didn't even want to look into the future. The whole experience made me look back at my own life, recalling how my psychic ability had shaped it, and how I had come to be the one who Jacqui had contacted after her murder. The 'why me?' questions started to enter my head again, as well as all the 'ifs' and 'buts'. If I hadn't been living in London, would she have come to me? If I hadn't foreseen deaths before, would I have seen hers? I had done my best, but what if there was more I could have done to help?

I had suffered some traumatic and disturbing experiences I wished I hadn't, and I felt very strongly that the disadvantages of my gift outweighed the benefits. In the time immediately after the police investigation, this was an issue that weighed heavily on my mind. I started to suffer quite badly from depression and I was tired of constantly seeing terrible things and not being able to do anything about them. I just wanted it to stop.

- CHAPTER 10 -

I HAD BEEN suffering these thoughts long before Jacqui came to me, but she was definitely the strongest emotional turmoil I faced. Looking back, even the build up to that time was full of upheaval, as if events were gradually intensifying until they reached that critical moment for me. The autumn of 1981, after Kathleen's death, was extremely upsetting and personally I had a very hard time. I have to thank my friends in the Spiritualist Churches for helping me through those terrible days. Without them I may not have been mentally able to cope with later events.

The Spiritualist Churches are beautiful. I was apprehensive at first to know what to make of them. Because I had been brought up in the shadow of the Catholic Church in Ireland, I had never experienced anything like them, or could ever hope to imagine the peace that was waiting there for me. The energy that comes from the sermons that the medium gives is full of philosophy; the spirit sends such lovely wisdom. Then you have the hymns and some lovely prayers and later on people meet up afterwards, have a cup of tea and they talk. People go into another room where they receive healing, and it is absolutely a beautiful experience where everyone is treated with the height of respect. After a while I began to give services myself. My first church service was in Ruislip Manor. It was a wonderful experience and I was very, very nervous that night, having to stand up in this church, hoping the spirits would not fail me, and would come with their blessings and messages.

I received some wonderful messages and that in itself gave me a great sense of fulfilment. The organisers were very pleased with my work. People were ringing up, talking to the head of the organisation, saying it had been a wonderful service. That was my first time on a platform and it had gone well for me, and for a time it felt good to be able to help and comfort people again by using the positive side of my ability. People rang looking for sittings, and came to me hoping to communicate with the spirit world.

After that I went on to hold several platforms in the local Spiritualist Church, and from there moved on to Wembley. The church there was packed. There was a woman who was very upset. It seemed that a young gentleman close to her had jumped under a train. I explained to her why he did it, what happened and where he was now. She was very upset that he had apparently jumped under a train. She didn't know that he was unhappy or sad, and I explained to her that actually what happened was that he had had a dizzy spell and fell, rather than jumped. That is what the spirit told me anyway, and I repeated that to her.

I don't believe in going to all these fairs and doing readings in hotels, but there is great respect in Church. I wouldn't work in a hall where somebody was drinking and bringing in cigarettes and smoking. I would have to work where there is pure, clean energy. True mediums will do this: they will work with pure clean energy.

England has quite a lot of Spiritualist Churches; nearly every town and village in England would have one. I even discovered one in the Isle of Man. Other countries like Ireland have very few; but the attitude towards spiritualism is changing and people are beginning to embrace and understand the spirit side a lot more.

❧ ❧ ❧ ❧ ❧

I MOVED ON with my life, I suppose, for a while, but Kathleen's death had knocked the heart out of me. I was finding it very hard to get back into my stride, but that is life; just when you are picking up and doing well and getting on your feet something comes along and knocks you down. This is one of the times in my life when I hit rock bottom and I stayed there for quite a long time. I remained in close contact with Kathleen's family, because she had been so close to me. There will always be that close contact there.

I continued going to my Spiritualist Circle and things were getting stronger and stronger, with my feelings getting more positive. I was amazed at some of the things I saw. I watched one of the other mediums go into a trance one night and a Chinese guy came through and spoke and another Indian person came through another medium. You could see the face change completely, their face disappeared and the Indian's face came out. Experiences were opening up around me.

Another time I went to see a transfiguration—that is when the person comes through the medium. My grandmother came through. I could hear her speaking to the medium and she told me that she was there for me and I wasn't to be disillusioned. I was to have trust. It was an amazing experience. Then another time we saw a film about poltergeists. It was a true story about poltergeists in this family's home in Essex. The psychics got together and went in, and it was real. You could see everything; there were no trick cameras. The woman was lifted from the bed and the cat was fired from the living room to the kitchen. It was very frightening. I wasn't to know that only a year down the road, an event was waiting to happen, which was much more terrifying for me than that incident in Essex.

I continued to practice being a medium, and out of darkness and despair I had suddenly rediscovered this wonderful spiritual power that I had. Somehow I could help people who were unhappy or who were stressed out or needed comfort. One of the lessons we learned about the work we do is the amount of people who come with broken spirit; it is like seeing a bird with a broken wing trying to fly. When I go to funerals I can see the pain and the hurt, the sadness that engulfs everybody at that particular time. I feel sad, and then I feel overwhelmed by that sadness.

One night a spirit guide came to me quite fed up and he explained to me all about his reasons for working with me. He explained that at times I would doubt myself, but he reminded me that I had learned a great deal. He said passages in my life would not always be easy. As a child I had had many strange dreams where I was told that my path through life would be very difficult for many years but that I would be able to find the peace that I had been searching for, so I thanked him for his message and he told me he would always be with me. He told me of the broken people who would come into my life and how they would reach out to me for my help, and at times I would feel much burdened by my gift and at other times I would feel very joyful for my gift. Sometimes you cannot give hope, you have to just pray and hope that a person will receive healing from the spirits above.

I was still learning about my own abilities, even if I wasn't always sure I wanted them. To the day I die

I will remember one particular reading, not because of any historic happening, but more in relation to my power to psychometrise objects. I discovered I could do this when going for an interview. I was speaking to the secretary, who had recently become engaged. Her ring was the centre of attention and the rest of the girls were busy trying it on and making a wish. I was offered the ring to try it on for luck, when suddenly I received flashes of the secretary's life. I was able to give her lots of information about her life and then I was surrounded by the girls who were pushing watches, chains, all kinds of jewellery at me for information.

That was certainly a new dimension for me and I have used it to good effect in my work. I use it mostly to help families whose sons and daughters have gone missing. One woman came to see me in quite an agitated state. She was not particularly interested in what I had to tell her, but was rather insistent that I would try and psychometrise what she removed from a paper bag instead. Once I got over the shock, I could see the funny side of things. I do whatever I can, but this woman came to me with her husband's underpants. She wanted me to try and see if he had been with another woman. I declined ... I said no, thank you very much, but I had to laugh.

Without knowing it I was still on the road to self-discovery, a road that was to bring me to a lot of different places and situations. There were times when I questioned myself and lost faith; I would eventually get it back, and I considered all this part of my learning. We must understand why our life has to go on; it cannot remain the same. Some people concentrate on the material world and worry about it so much that it takes over and the spirit life is forgotten, finished with. This is one of the reasons why we find it hard to have peace of mind. There is room for both and it is important to make room to keep a balance in life. If you work hard on the spiritual side of things and tune into the spiritual side through meditation you will find that you will get the strength to understand any misfortune that might come your way. You will also respect any good luck that comes your way if you want to call it that, but the spirit world has neither good nor bad luck; they call it lessons and blessings, and there is a difference. At the time, of course, I didn't know this.

I learned a great deal, and I enjoyed most of the lessons that life offered me. Some of them I wasn't happy about at all. Though I had friends, I was never completely comfortable with my lot in life. I had always disliked being seen as unusual in any way, which is why I tried to keep my gift a secret from new people, and it was very hard to fit in with any one group of friends. Yet at the same time, I think sometimes I actually used my work to escape a social life.

My love life was always a bit of a disaster. I tended to put all my heart and soul into work and being committed to looking after people, so maybe

I didn't leave enough for someone to look after me. I had been involved in relationships and I had met people I had cared for very much. I was always an all or nothing person, and I met people who were the same way. I suppose I threw myself into taking care of other people's problems because deep down inside I didn't know how to take care of my own.

It is very hard to have a long term relationship if you continually pick the wrong type of person. You have to know the person you are going out with wants what you want. If they don't there is no point in hanging on in the hope that he or she will change. If it is not working you move on because you are damaging your spirit, you are damaging your soul's powers to be happy. I recognised all of this, and I met some very amazing people in my spiritual groups who were psychic like myself and had wonderful gifts, but I didn't meet anyone who wanted exactly what I did. Some people were very spiritual, very psychic, and I knew that some day they would recognise their own gifts fully, when they had travelled the road I had. Still, nobody told me it was going to be easy. On the contrary, they all told me it was going to be hard.

As I progressed in the Spiritualist Circles, along with the others, we each received messages and learned a great deal from each other. It was a wonderful experience. One of the most comforting and enjoyable aspects of this was that I was actually secure in the knowledge that I was with people who knew and understood me. It was when I went out to a night club or a disco or a party and I met people that I would tend to shy away from them. I mean, it was very hard to say to somebody, 'Hi, my name is Christine, I speak to the dead.' I couldn't do that. I used to tell everyone I was a hairdresser. In the end, I had lots of people ringing me up wanting their hair cut, but I couldn't cut my nails, let alone someone's hair.

Eventually, of course, after a while, people knew what I did for a living and they were okay about it. They actually were better about it than I had expected, but it was difficult for me when I was young and out in a nightclub. I'd meet a young guy who would say, 'What do you do for a living?' and I'd tell him I could read his future or his mind. It is a little bit daunting.

Then there are the people that will challenge you, like when they ask, 'What am I thinking about?'

I said to one guy, 'Whatever it is you are thinking you can keep your thoughts to yourself.'

It was obvious what he was thinking; you didn't have to be a psychic to work that one out.

♧ ♧ ♧ ♧ ♧

1983 WAS AGAIN a very strong year for me, pulling my life together again after the death of Kathleen. A lot of things happened in my life. I became more and more engrossed in the spirit world and I joined a second circle in Ealing and found it very interesting. For me this was something new, as it was a healing circle. A group of psychics and mediums came together from different circles, each one in need of healing.

When you are involved in the spirit world you are constantly giving through your work and can find yourself drained, physically as well as emotionally. There is just so much happening in the world; we read about it in the newspapers, we see it on the television, and as well as gaining healing for the individual, other mediums hold healing circles where they concentrate on areas in the world where there is darkness and despair and people are suffering. There are places where people suffer incredible pain, as well as emotional loss. War brings with it terrible destruction, and peoples' lives have to be put back together, not to mention their homes and towns. I was fascinated to see the healing circles at work. They concentrate together, sending light into places where there is sadness, and into areas that need healing.

I learned so much at the healing circle. You learn about different areas of healing. Some people heal through thought, others by the laying on of hands. For years the Catholic Church did not agree with the alternative methods and healers, but today it has become much more acceptable and they will allow lay people to do hands-on healing. Gradually, slowly, it is all getting there and it is all happening, but the spirit world has been around for a very long time. Spirituality, prayers, the lovely energy that is there to help people heal, is there. People are beginning to recognise that. It is sad that there has to be so much pain in the world before people can recognise the beauty, wisdom and love of the spiritual side of life.

Love is a bridge that joins us together with those we cannot live without. Remember, it is only a bridge of time that is between us and the people we love in spirit. They are not gone forever, nor are we going to stay in this world forever. That is one thing we have to be very sure of; we are not all going to be in control of the time or the place when we leave.

Many do choose when they will leave this world, however. Most of those decisions are made in the depths of depression, resulting in death by suicide. Thousands of people are killed tragically in accidents. Hundreds are killed on our roads every year. But by far the worst way to leave this world is when your life is taken from you violently by an act of murder. The act of murder takes away all control over your hopes and dreams for the future and in reality destroys not only the victim's life forever but that of the extended family, who are left to suffer on long after the murder of a loved one.

So it was for Jacqui, who that year lost her right to life through a dreadful act of violence. Her life was cut short just as she was reaching out for a fresh start. Her untimely death left her in a state of shock in the spirit world and her family absolutely devastated by their loss, and for 20 years her pain and suffering was to haunt me too. I had used all the skills and gifts at my disposal to try to help her find justice, and to rest in peace, but the fact that the case was not solved weighed heavily on me.

- CHAPTER 11 -

AFTER JACQUI HAD first visited me, as with everything, time moved on and by 1986 both my sister Mary and I were more able to cope with her appearances and disruptions. Jacqui was still with me constantly, venting her anger at the man who had killed her, and was living freely each and every day. I tried to listen to her, but what more could I do? I was incredibly upset and traumatized by what had happened, and I needed to find a way out of it. I needed to start living like a normal person, to enjoy a normal life and have normal experiences, because I wasn't sure how much more I would be able to take. Soon enough though, things would get even worse.

While I was living back in Ruislip, I started to make a living from doing readings for people. I had met a lot of influential people, and at times it was strange to be picked up in a limousine outside my flat, when I couldn't even afford driving lessons, to be brought to huge mansions where I would meet ambassadors, members of the Arabian royal family, and of the Egyptian government. But I was still very upset and down about my circumstances, the death of loved ones, and the traumatic feeling of knowing these things were going to happen long before they did. I decided to stop practising as a medium, in the hope that I would stop seeing visions.

I got a job at an RAF base, but told nobody about my abilities. As far as I could see, all it brought was misery. I wanted a complete break from it. I wanted to be myself with no more spirit interruptions. I was working in the hangar where the soldiers used to come in during the war. The POWs were brought to RAF Northolt where there is a memorial in their name today. I was busy working one morning, and afterwards I washed my hands. I turned off the tap and when I looked back the tap was on again. Then I heard footsteps as if someone was next to me. Next the tap was turned on and off again. I said to myself, *This is getting ridiculous*. I could not understand it; lights were going on and off at the same time. I thought I saw a flash go by one of the mirrors and I thought, *Oh no, not again. I don't want this to happen to me again.*

I thought that by going to Northolt I could take a break from all of that. It wasn't that simple. It seemed that wherever I went the spirits came too. I remember looking around; I could hear the ghosts coming and going. I tried to push it to one side out of my mind. The next thing I knew I looked around and there was an airman dressed in the old type RAF uniform with a rucksack on his back. He came and looked around and walked straight through the wall in front of me. It continued for a few minutes and another airman came in. He walked the same way in and through the wall. At least four came in and walked straight through the wall in front of me. These visions were intense and deeply moving. They scared me, but I had come to accept them as part of my life. My experiences were not just going to be restricted to the Spiritualist Churches or the Spiritualist Circle; they were everywhere I went again. They were inside me. There was no escape from the spirits. I did not want to tell anyone what had happened. I didn't think that anyone would believe me, but I got talking to one of the lads one day, one of the older ones, about different things. He told me about how the airmen came in during the war to refuel and various other tasks. He told me that the hangar was haunted. I just looked at him and said, 'Oh, fancy that.'

I made some good friends there and remember one weekend going down to visit one particular girl called Ann who I got on very well with. I had described to her what kind of house she was going to end up living in, and shortly after that she lived in a cottage that fitted the description I had given her, with her husband Paul and her dog Sam. There was a lovely walkway just beside the house, and shortly after arriving, laughing and joking, Ann and I headed off together for a walk around her new property. We were both having a great time catching up on each other's lives and chatting about this and that until suddenly, as we walked down the laneway, I froze. I saw a horrible vision that sent a shudder through me. I was reluctant to go into what I had seen but felt it was of the utmost importance to warn Ann. I sensed that somebody was going to be murdered in that very laneway—a woman with blonde hair, out walking her dog—and because Ann was blonde, and had a dog, I had to warn her never to walk that way again.

'Please don't ever risk it,' I said to her, 'because Sam won't be able to help you.'

I could see I had frightened her, but I made her promise to never walk down there again. Within a year, a blonde woman who had been out walking her dog was found suffering severe head injuries after a savage attack in the very lane where I had foreseen it. She died soon afterwards in the hospital. I was glad I had helped a close friend, but I wished these terrible visions had not returned. They seemed to be ruining any good times I was able to enjoy.

One day, my little family, eager to have as normal a life as other families did in the summer months, decided to have a barbecue. After all, it was June and the weather was perfect, a really beautiful day, and we were all excited. I went up to the local shop to run a few errands and to get the finishing touches for our little event. That day in June had held the promise of so much fun but, in fact, it turned out to be one of the most traumatic days of my life. I woke up that morning with a sense of unease all around me, leaving me not quite knowing what was wrong, but I tried to forget about it as we had such a fun day planned. It is hard to imagine how I could be happy on the one hand and excited about planning our day out, and on the other be filled with a feeling of dread slowly gnawing at me in the pit of my stomach; a feeling that always meant bad news for someone.

Kathleen had visited me a few weeks before, and seemed distressed, but I wasn't sure why. I tried to ignore the feelings of dread and busied myself with the preparations. That morning at about 11.30am I got a phone call, and with it came news that was to change my life forever. My mother's neighbour, at home in Ireland, was on the other end of the line and had called to tell me to come home as soon as possible. I asked her why. There was a long silence on the line and then she said, 'I am sorry but Martin is dead, your brother was found dead this morning and your parents need you to come home.'

I dropped the phone and I screamed and screamed. My sister ran in and in the middle of my screams I tried to tell her that Martin was dead. I sat down and tried to calm myself. I screamed with such intensity that my friend Jane ran down from upstairs and my friend Eddie who was on his way to work called in to see what was wrong. The death hit me hard. In the midst of my despair I instantly recalled those three times in my life when I had had the exact same dream, and in each one of those dreams I had passed an old derelict house, and saw a rope hanging. I asked an unseen bystander in my dream, 'What has happened?' and each time the reply came back, 'It is your brother Martin, he has taken his life and he has passed over. Thy will be done.'

Each dream was identical, so when I calmed down I rang back to Ireland and tried to find out more. Mrs O'Neill, our neighbour, didn't want to tell me. She said there had been an accident. I said to her on the phone, 'Did Martin take his life? Did Martin hang himself?'

After a time, it seemed a long silence, too long, she said yes. It was in the grounds of The Hall where we used to play. My nightmare had finally come true. Suddenly it was my reality.

I had woken up that morning to a beautiful sunny June day preparing for a barbecue, and instead by lunchtime I was preparing for a funeral. The banks were closed; there was no way to get money to come home, so I rang a friend of mine who said she would get us home by ferry. At that point I really didn't feel that I could cope with a journey on a boat, so I rang another friend of mine, a new acquaintance who worked for British Airways. I explained the situation and asked if there would be any way we could get three airline tickets and pay at the other side.

She told us to wait. She would be back to us in half an hour. She phoned back later and she had three one-way tickets for us from Heathrow Airport to Dublin, so our journey home began. It was the most painful journey of my life. Little did I know then that my time in England, my life there was over. It had finished, all in one day. We returned to Ireland, and arrived in Dublin with very heavy hearts, Mary and I locked in our own grief.

This is one of the most painful memories of my life, the hardest part of my story I have to tell. Martin and I were very close. We grew up together, we shared a lot of dreams, and there was a lot of me that felt a special closeness to my brother. Our childhood was a very special part of our lives, and I fondly remember every little thing about him.

When he was smaller, Martin was in a special school in Baldoyle, a little village just off the Coast Road in Dublin. He had been sent there to get help for a speech impediment. He hated it there and we hated him being there, but eventually we brought him home. There was a special bond between myself and Martin, and that made his parting even more difficult.

The journey home to Dublin after Martin's death was a nightmare. When I wasn't filled up with tears and pain I was flooded with flashbacks, memories of us as children when we would sit on the bed and listen to Elvis Presley, or lie across the bed

and watch the Curragh lights twinkle, and dream
of far away places and times to come. Sadly when
I went to England, Martin missed me very much
and I missed him too, but we were always close at
heart, our thoughts were always of each other, and
I always enjoyed coming home. We would meet up
and go for long walks and we would talk as if we
had never been apart.

Martin's funeral was huge. Several hundred
people attended. If only he had realised how much
he was loved. My father was 72 at the time and my
mother was 70. In and around that time my father
was a fairly active man for his age, who still rode a
bike, and my mother could still walk a mile a day,
but his death broke them. Overnight, their spirits
were broken and I watched them crumble. Their
lives would never be the same again, and in fact,
none of our lives ever were. That is the tragic thing
about suicide; it destroys so many people. It is such
a sad and lonely passing and it robs families of a last
farewell. It robs them of a chance to try and talk to
somebody, to tell them that they are loved.

The night I came home was the worst night ever,
with the thunder and lightning frightening in its
intensity. Every light in Stradbally had gone out;
the lightning had caused terrible damage. It felt
that the spirits were angry that such a wonderful
soul had been taken and had been forced to leave
this earth. Most people are very generous and open
with their hearts and very caring and comforting,
and I will never forget that. I cannot forget that,

but there was a small group, who were causing pain in the first place, who had continued to be abusive to Martin. When I came home I was full of anger. I had never felt such anger in my life, and I was beginning to truly understand the kind of anger and despair Jacqui felt.

I know now that it is through the suffering and pain that I suffered after losing Martin that makes it possible for me to help others. It is not until you actually experience the tragedy of suicide and untimely death that you can understand the pain particular to it. An accident would have been bad enough, but with suicide you are always left thinking: *If only I had known what he was thinking, then I could have made a difference.*

I found out then that while I was living in England, a group of local lads from Stradbally had bullied Martin, making his life a misery just because he was a little different, and this just increased my anger. I put it down to ignorance and boredom, but it still infuriated me. I told them off in my own way, trying to make them understand the consequences of their actions. I wasn't trying to blame them for Martin's death, just trying to make them realise the pain their words had caused him.

At that time in my life I had become very angry, and very bitter. I felt hurt and I felt angry and I felt sad. Grief, anger and bitterness are all part of the one thing, and they all come from a pain inside— the injustice that you feel, that somebody has been through so much pain. I used to visit the location where Martin died for a while, in what had been the most wonderful place for me—The Hall—and leave flowers there, but he came to me and told me not to, as it was only making me sad. I sensed he didn't want me to go there any more so I stopped.

I did return to England after getting through my initial anger, but I went through a lot of difficulties. I found it hard to pray, and I found I wanted to be on my own a lot. I must have lit thousands of candles and I still couldn't find peace of mind, still couldn't get away from the pain and the hurt and the anger I felt inside. Watching my parents, watching their sadness, watching my father cry every day was so painful. I had been through a lot of hurt in my life but this was one of the worst times.

That is why I understand, why I have a sense of compassion for anybody who comes to me who is in pain, anyone who has lost a loved one through suicide, through accidents, through murder. People who commit suicide are sad, their life is empty, they are lonely, they are hurting inside, and cannot take the hurt that life throws at them any more. After the passing of somebody under traumatic circumstances, let it be either suicide or accident or murder or whatever the circumstances may be, the people left behind find it impossible to understand. There are always questions, and the one question on everyone's lips is: Why?

There is always a sense of guilt, anger, frustration, loneliness. The loneliest feeling in the world is when you are grieving for a person you have lost.

After the launch of my first book, I sent a copy to actor
William Roach of *Coronation Street*. Imagine my delight
when he wrote to me inviting me onto the set. My sister
Mary came along for a visit.

Vera McHugh (left), wrote this book with me. Here we are
launching the first editon of the book.

Jacqui Poole, the beautiful young woman who had her life taken away from her by a cold and ruthless murderer.
© *Author's own collection*

Above and right: The flat where Jaqui was murdered in 1983. It was located a few miles from where I lived in Ruislip.

Below: The gardens at Ickenham, where Jacqui's killer, Anthony 'Pokie' Ruark, is alleged to have temporarily hidden the jewellery he callously stole from her flat, even taking the rings from her fingers.

A thorough search of the area, including the laneway leading to Jacqui's flat at Lakeside Close, was made by police, but little evidence could be found. Suspecting 'Pokie' Ruark, the police made a rough sketch (below) of the gardens, road and buildings near his home.

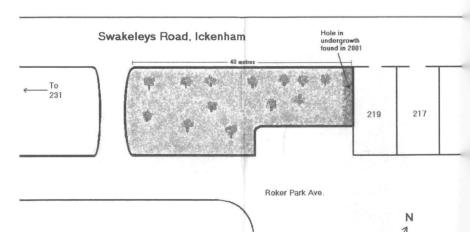

Swakeleys Road, Ickenham

Hole in undergrowth found in 2001

← To 231

40 metres

219   217

Roker Park Ave.

N

Detectives Tony Batters (above right) and Andy Smith showed amazing understanding and patience towards me, even though I am sure they had never come across a story like mine before. I met Andy Smith (above) after 23 years, and we got on great with each other.

 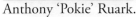

Anthony 'Pokie' Ruark.

I went into a trance and, with Jacqui's spirit guiding me, scrawled the killer's nickname on a notepad.

From left: Me, Nanny Norton (a family friend), Mammy and my sister Mary. There is a history of the 'sixth sense' in my family; my mother was always very sure of signs in her dreams.

My nephew and godson Canice has always remained very close to me. I lived with him in England when Jacqui Poole's ghost started visiting me.

Stradbally, County Laois, is my home, a place where I will always feel welcome and at peace. I love going to the music festival, *Electric Picnic*, which takes place there every year.

My mother and father are pictured here with my cousin, Kathleen. I had a premonition about Kathleen's death, but despite my efforts, I was unable to prevent it.

On the day Ruark was sentenced, Jacqui's spirit came to me in a way she had never visited before: she was radiant, full of joy and completely at peace as she floated above my bed and thanked me for all that I had done. To see her at peace made everything I had gone through worthwhile, and brought an end to the ordeal that had lasted 18 years.

It is a different type of loneliness from missing a friend who has gone away. It hurts the soul; it goes deep. I felt such loneliness over Martin, but with that I was still being visited by Jacqui, and I could feel her desperation and anger even more. She was suffering the very same feelings, but they were for her own life, which had been taken away from her. Again I just felt so distraught that she could not find peace.

The autumn of 1986, just after my brother died, was extremely upsetting and was a very hard time for me. For a while I really couldn't do any more psychic work, because I simply didn't want to do it. I wasn't able to handle it. There was no way I could sit down and do spirit or psychic readings for people. I just had to close the door temporarily. The way I felt at that time, I never wanted to work with the spirits again. I was angry with them. I was angry with God. I was angry with almost everybody. Strangely, while all of this was closing in on me, and while I didn't realise it at the time, I was probably closer to Jacqui then than I had been for quite some time. Our anger was all-encompassing.

I wasn't angry with Martin though, because I know what it is like to hurt. I went through very deep despairing moments when I could have done the same thing too, so I knew what it was like. I know what it is like to be at the very edge; it only takes one little thing to push you over. I have been there so I understand the despair, the pain, the hurt, the sadness. I know the awful feeling of emptiness. I have been down that road so I do understand.

❊ ❊ ❊ ❊ ❊

THAT YEAR I stayed home with my parents after I realised I didn't want to be in London anymore. I had been living a different life there. I was starting to earn money, I had a little car, my life was finally coming together. Before Martin's death I was starting to feel happy or at least trying to get my life together after Jacqui, when all of a sudden I was back to getting £16.50 on the dole in Ireland. It was an indefinite plan. I had no plans to actually stay in Ireland. At some stage I felt I would go back.

It took from June to October to get the inquest into Martin's death organised. It takes a long time to get an inquest in Ireland. Everything is always done very slowly. They are two different worlds, Ireland and England, two very different countries, two totally different worlds, yet we are only 55 minutes away on a plane journey. The inquest would open the pain all over again but eventually things started settling down a little bit and I was able to make some progress, with the help of a couple of very good friends who helped me through it.

I eventually ended up on a FÁS course, Ireland's training and development scheme, and then found myself involved in local politics, gradually regaining a foothold in the community and my life. Soon enough though, my old life started to come back to me. I met a woman in Portlaoise. I don't really know how it came about but somehow I ended up reading her cards, and from there it spiralled. Every week she would have a crowd, with a few girls for me. Each time I went to her shop, there would be people waiting for readings. She would let me earn a few pounds for myself, which was very nice. When I did spirit readings in England I was earning at least £20, but when I came home after Martin died I was able to get maybe £5 for a sitting or tarot reading, so the drop was considerable.

Here I was back in Ireland, and what a change in my financial standing! Sometimes you have to start all over again, and that was what I did. I was lucky enough to be invited to give readings to a group, mostly ladies, in one of their homes in Portlaoise. Then my friend called one day and told me she was moving to Dublin. She got my name on the lease of her building, and gave me the deposit for the rent. She was a wonderful human being.

I didn't have an appointments system; people would just come in off the street, and news spread through word of mouth. I could have a couple this week and I could have a few more next week and I used to go to visit people's houses. Before I knew it my name had spread all around; there were quite a lot of people coming from Portlaoise and they were coming from a little further afield. Gradually over a period of time people found me and I became established, you might say.

It was around the early 90s, when I was finding my feet again, when the terrible cases of the numerous missing people in Ireland started to get a lot of attention, and rumours were abound that there was a serial killer on the loose. When it comes to missing women in Ireland it brings me more pain than I can tell. Various women had vanished in an area around Leinster, which encompassed Laois.

One woman went missing very close to where I lived, and I got a strong sense of where she was, but I was not involved in the case and really wasn't sure if I wanted to be. In a separate incident, a man had disappeared on his way home one night. I knew when I was asked to tune into his spirit that it wasn't foul play. Something had happened on his way home. He just got confused and lost his way. We went looking for him, but he had told me himself that he would be found on Wednesday, and it was on Wednesday at 10.30 am that he was found. He was quite a character actually. I got very fond of him. We actually seemed to get fond of each other. He still had a sense of humour. A few of us who were looking for him were sitting round talking on the Sunday just before he was found and all of a sudden the lights went on and off and everybody just looked, and he laughed and he said it wasn't him, the bulb had blown.

'I didn't do that', he said to me. It was just a coincidence. But you should have seen everybody's faces. When he had been found and when we had gone to the funeral he told me in the church that they had forgotten to put his shoes on, so I told his nephew.

'He said you forgot his shoes.'

'Oh my God I knew I forgot something,' he said, shocked.

Annie McCarrick, a young American student living here was the first of the actual 'vanished', who just seemed to disappear without a trace. There was a massive hunt for her and the media coverage hit saturation point at the time, but all to no avail. For a year before Annie went missing I was enduring awful nightmares involving women being murdered. I kept waking up in a sweat. These dreadful images kept on coming and because I did not receive enough information to do anything, I tried to block the memories. When I heard the details of a case reported in the media, for me it was a case of *déjà vu*. I was feeling a lot of strange things I hadn't felt in a while, perhaps because of the very close proximity of the cases. It got to a stage that I just became very distraught and concerned, but I didn't know why. Then all of a sudden the first woman was reported missing and it all became clear.

I always visualised Annie somewhere very scenic, where there is a park, and I still sense she is in the area of the Wicklow to Dublin Mountains, where people probably walk past, going into a picnic area. I sensed that. Many more have since gone missing.

I was very reluctant to get involved in these cases in any way, after what I had experienced with

Jacqui, and also after the death of my brother and the questions that had raised for me. I also felt I was back almost to square one as regards people's opinions as me as a psychic. I did offer my services though, and at times I was asked to help. Even when I wasn't involved directly, I felt that I was, because I was still seeing these visions and had these tortured souls coming to me looking for help.

I had a dream of a girl who was in a wooded area one night, which left me very disturbed. It was horrible to see and to have playing over in my head. In my dream there was a dark coloured jeep with a man driving it. The girl was constantly asking for someone to help her. It seems that she had trusted him and could not understand why no one could hear her cries for help. The reason why she couldn't be heard is because she had already been murdered. She had passed over and was totally unaware of it.

In the dream the man driving the jeep stopped at the side of the road where there was either a fountain or a pump. There was a garage a short way up the road. The girl left the jeep and ran for her life, heading for the garage looking for help. She was so pleased that she had reached the garage safely and called out to a fair-haired chap who was coming around the side of the building.

He got a terrible shock, and in my dream, he told his friends later that he really did see the ghost of a beautiful young woman that day, running towards him, pleading for him to help her. Meanwhile the driver of the jeep washed the muck from his shoes at the pump, his evil deed already done.

I have had strange visions from time to time from some of the missing women, one in particular whom I shall not name. She has sent me clear pictures at least three times. She can give me a good description of the journey that she took with her abductor in his van. She ended up in a large house that she thought was being renovated as men came and spoke to him through an open window. She just drifted into my mind last summer. Again there is insufficient material to go to the Gardaí with.

Another young woman with long dark hair, about 27 years old, who passed over in tragic circumstances came to me twice, gave me no details, then left. What happens is that when someone is either abducted and held or actually murdered, the victim can only send out images of where they are at that particular time. For instance, they could be in the boot of a car and all that they can transmit is their sense of fear and pain but the picture is dark and of no help to anyone. Once more these are the times that I can consider my gift a curse, when I can only receive fragments of the picture and feel all the pain and anguish, yet it is enough to last two lifetimes.

I FOUND IT very hard to settle back into Ireland when I came home first; the narrow mindedness of a smaller country upset me. I had been living in a multi-racial country where people were allowed to live and do their own thing, within reason. Now I was back in Ireland where everyone wanted to know what you had for breakfast and everybody thinks there is something strange about you if you happen to have an ability or talent beyond the norm.

I wasn't sure if I was being taken seriously or being seen as a sort of curio. Mary Fanning of RTE interviewed me on my psychic work and on the work connected with the missing women of Ireland. I told her what I believe; that we have two serial killers in our midst. There are a lot of very good mediums in Ireland who would be quite happy to sit around in a group with the police and work confidentially with them, as I have done in England, but there is a lot of scepticism from both the gardaí, who are starting to come around, and from the public. But we would like the opportunity to help find these missing women and put an end to the suffering of their families. That is another area that is being considered by many mediums. With Jacqui it was completely different for me. She propelled herself into my life and the images she gave me were more than enough to convince a judge, but I couldn't relay them.

I spoke to Mary on *Nationwide* and I was also interviewed on other programmes about my gift because more and more people had heard about me. On the one hand I was wary and didn't want to get as close as I had done with Jacqui, whose visits were finally starting to peter out until finally she stopped coming to me, but on the other I wanted to help people who needed answers.

Sometimes I ask myself: *Will this curse ever leave me*? I had a dream or vision this one night and in the dream my little town of Stradbally was grieving. Three coffins were lying in the church. That was all that came through; the terrible sadness in the town and the three coffins. I put this vision away from me as I did not know what the message was, and I didn't want to know.

A short time later, even though I never give readings in a pub, one night I received a warning for a young man and felt compelled to speak to him. I realise now that when I get a message I should never try to understand it with the logical side of my brain, which in this instance is exactly what I did. The message was to warn this young man and, as I knew that he bought and sold cars, I thought logically that the warning was about one of his deals. This was in September and my dream of the three coffins was a year previously. Just as my vision showed me, in November there were three coffins standing side by side in the church as a result of a horrific crash.

There were four young men in the car, and only one of them survived. I was very good friends with one of the chaps who lost his life that night. He knew what I did for a living. He never once joked or laughed at my profession. He always trusted and believed in me and he often asked me for advice. All three lads came back to me after he passed over. He was hoping that their deaths would be a warning to other young people to slow down or take a taxi. I saw the grief and the pain of the families, and it was just unbearable. They have to go up to the graveyard every Christmas Day to say Happy Christmas to their sons, standing over their graves. It was a real tragedy and it shook the people of the town to the very core. At times like these I wish that side of my psyche did not work.

There was a situation where a young woman went missing and her body turned up nine days later in the river. I knew in my heart she hadn't committed suicide, as did her mother, but that's they way it looked. The facts were broadcast for all to see, causing the girl's family untold pain and suffering. All I could do was assure the woman that her daughter had not taken her life, but the pain of knowing that she had been murdered resulted in the woman taking her own life a few years later. She just couldn't take the injustice of her daughter's life having been taken away. A few high profile cases came my way in this time, and I became involved with the families of some people. One person who came to me for a reading was from the family of a very well known woman who was in prison for the murder of her husband. The husband was on the other side, and was very angry. When the woman was sentenced to life for his murder, he was very much at peace. He felt justice had finally been done. The family felt relieved at this news, and I was glad

I was able to help. I was becoming quite used to my life, helping people, but from a safe distance, and things were going fairly well for me. I didn't really get any indication that my life was once more going to change dramatically, which I suppose is strange for a psychic, but I'm sure nobody could ever imagine themselves in the situation I was about to find myself in.

- CHAPTER 13 -

JACQUI HAD NOT visited me for quite some time, but the very thought or mention of her name at any stage made it possible for me to relive her ordeal and all the anguish felt after her case was unsolved. She had pleaded with me to try something else, another avenue to find justice for her, but I felt like I had failed her and that feeling was not going to go away. Poor Jacqui; she had traversed that great divide after her shocking death, to find peace so that she could rest in eternity, but her pain at getting nowhere, even after she had identified her killer, left her in a sort of hell.

I put her into the back of my brain as much as I could, as other matters took over in my life. In the summer of 2001, I was attending the local hospital in Portlaoise and was awaiting my turn to see the doctor. For some reason I looked up at the glass doors of the laboratory in front of me, and got a shock. I was sure I saw a fleeting image of a young woman with blonde hair on the other side of the door. I looked again, and there in the reflection, clear as day, was Jacqui's face. I was intrigued and got up and went through the door to see why she was there, but she was gone. Because I hadn't thought about her for quite a while, I couldn't help but wonder: *What is she doing here?* It shook me, and got me thinking back to that story I thought had finished.

I had a dream one night shortly after that, that left me a little confused. I knew it was a psychic dream because every detail was as fresh when I woke up as it had been while I slept. What bothered me was the unusual nature of the dream. I saw no one and could hear no one speak. I only saw a pair of hands, and someone trying very hard to remove some rings from them, but couldn't figure out what it meant. I don't know why, but I just didn't think of Jacqui at the time. Looking back, it seems so obvious now, but I suppose I had been trying hard to keep her out of my mind and I honestly thought, or hoped, my life had moved on from that dreadful time. As far as I was concerned that chapter of my life was over.

Not long after that, I received a phone call from my sister Mary in England. She was very excited and could hardly wait to tell me her good news. The Jacqueline Poole murder case had been re-opened, and 'Pokie' Ruark had been arrested again, 17 years after he was first taken into custody. I couldn't believe it. I was over the moon with delight, and it was only then that the penny dropped in relation to the dream I had and the vision of Jacqui in the hospital. Batters had apparently come looking for 'the Irish medium' who had helped so much on the original case back in 1983, and had found Mary. He had kept every file and kept tabs on the developments in the only unsolved case he had worked on, even after he retired. Mary gave him my number then and he phoned me to tell me about the trial and to remain silent about any involvement in the case until it was all over. I had no problem in complying with his request, but I couldn't believe it—a chapter of my life I had hoped and prayed would close forever was now wide open again, and maybe, just maybe, there was a chance for Jacqui to find justice after all.

As it turned out, several high-profile murder cases had been re-opened in England due to significant developments in the area of forensic science. Jacqui's family had been campaigning to Detective Chief Inspector Norman McKinlay for the re-investigation of the case and because of the huge developments in forensics involving DNA, and because an informant named somebody else as Jacqui's murderer, the police were prompted to look at all the evidence again. McKinlay had sought out all of the original forensic items taken from the scene, the victim, and the suspect's clothes, and had sent them for examination.

The police then had to find Tony 'Pokie' Ruark. He had moved from Ruislip to Cirencester, Gloucestershire in the years after the murder, but had become involved in car crime and came to the attention of the National Crime Squad. He was put on the DNA database in 2000 after he was arrested for stealing £1,000 from his employer, and was convicted in March of that year, and sent to prison. The police could then run tests on his DNA samples to see if they could find a match.

In the process of re-investigating the evidence collected back in 1983, the police looked at the jumper they had found in Ruark's bin. I had told them they should keep any clothes he was trying to get rid of. I wasn't sure why, but I knew that an item of clothing would provide the key to him being convicted.

The jumper was examined using the latest in DNA technology; a technique known as Low Copy Number, which allowed the police to trace and examine a DNA profile from very small traces of DNA. Swabs taken from Jacqui and various items belonging to suspects at the time of the murder were stored away until now, and as soon as they were analysed, the lab came back to DCI McKinlay with a definite match to Jacqui. 'Pokie' Ruark was arrested and charged. The jumper he had thrown away had tiny traces of Jacqui's DNA on it, and under her fingernails there were traces of his skin.

He was brought to court almost 20 years after he had committed the crime. He must have thought he had got away with it.

Ruark knew he had been caught, but he was a cold man and he kept his cool throughout the second investigation. He completely changed his story and claimed that he had been having an affair with Jacqui, which would explain any traces of his DNA found on her clothing. The police were having none of this though, and proved that the numerous traces of Ruark's DNA on Jacqui's clothing indicated violence as opposed to intimacy. At the trial in 2001, when the DNA evidence was shown, Batter's report revealed that 'the findings were completely conclusive, identifying numerous exchanges of body fluids, skin cells and clothing fibres between the victim and the killer.'

The chances of error were quoted in the court as less than one in one billion. It looked like science had finally caught up with the evidence I had provided and so the police were able to prove Ruark's guilt.

Still, Ruark had tried to lie his way out of it. He claimed that he had left Jacqui safely that night and that one of her 'other lovers' must have killed her. This was sheer malice, rubbing salt into the wounds of her family by dragging Jacqui's name and reputation through the dirt. Her brother Terry, whose name she had called out in desperation in her last moments, attended every day of the trial and had to stand by and listen to Ruark slander

Jacqui. He was angered by some of the things said, mistakenly, during the two week trial and outside the courtrooms was determined to set the record straight. Contrary to what was being said in court, Jacqui was not a 'good time girl, just an affectionate and fun-loving woman', and that, 'Ruark was not her boyfriend, not her lover, just a member of the same social group.' His face clouding over, according to local media reporters, he added, 'And he sexually assaulted her and robbed her of life. Ruark has had 18 years of freedom that he should not have had, but this is finally justice after 18 years of waiting.'

On the morning that Ruark was sentenced in the Old Bailey, 24 August 2001, I had woken up early and was just lying there thinking about the day ahead when my room was suddenly filled with something like an extra bright sunshine that was almost blinding. When my eyes became accustomed to the intense light, I saw a beautiful vision of Jacqui. She was a very different woman to the one who had come to me all those years ago. She was floating over my bed, with the most radiant smile on her face as she drifted off towards the light.

It was a beautiful, departing vision of a tortured soul finally finding peace, and I felt so relieved and happy for her. I was so grateful for that image. There had been no need for words; she was at peace and had finally released her ties with this world. A lot of my doubts about my gift disappeared there and then, and I realised that I really had to cherish my ability to help others when nobody else could. It had taken a long time, but finally, the information I had given the police about the murder had paid off. On the day of sentencing, the trial judge Kenneth Machin summarised by saying: 'This was a brutal murder of a defenceless woman who had been nothing but kind to you.'

'Pokie' Ruark was sentenced to life in prison and Jacqui finally had her justice.

♣ ♣ ♣ ♣ ♣

AFTER THE TRIAL, Batters phoned me again and asked if I would go back to England. He told me then what I knew in my heart already; that the information I had given to the two detectives all those years ago was completely accurate and correct, and had convinced the police that they had their man. They just couldn't prove it through any admissible evidence. Absolutely everything I had told them had been checked and validated and left the police in no doubt that 'Pokie' Ruark had killed Jacqui, and in the way I had described. That was why Batters had looked so shocked at my information, after initially appearing sceptical.

The list of correct pieces of information was staggering, according to the police. How could I get it wrong? Tony said he wanted to fill in the few remaining blanks for me.

He had already spoken to a woman called Barbara Fisher, a local journalist who wrote for the local newspaper near Ruislip, the *Uxbridge & West*

Drayton Gazette, and both of them were looking forward to the meeting. I made a short trip over in September, and was happy to do so. There are no words to describe the feelings I experienced at the knowledge that Pokie was behind bars. I hugged myself several times on my journey and I am quite sure that anyone looking in my direction would have thought I was mad.

Though I was happy and excited, I was full of apprehension at the thought of meeting this police officer who had spoken to me all those years ago, and I was hoping that I would recognise him, and he me. When I stepped from the train at Uxbridge station, there he was, standing with his newspaper under his arm, complete with his pipe. It is funny how these little images remain. It was a joyful occasion. He escorted me to a coffee shop, where I met Barbara. She was so interested in my end of the story, and like every good journalist was pleased to have the inside track. Apparently, everyone wanted to speak to this unknown Irish medium. It was fascinating listening to Barbara and Batters recount the trial. They told me what everybody had said—the judge, the prosecutor and defence, Jacqui's family—and also how the police had finally caught up with Ruark using new forensic methods. It all sounded very complicated but I was interested to hear it explained. It was such a good feeling to listen to the banter between the two and to know that somehow I had helped Jacqui. I sometimes think that it was the angels who brought Jacqui's troubled soul to me for help. She had been murdered in February and not buried until June, and the thought of this poor soul wandering free, crying out for justice, made me sad. At least she had found me. I am sure the fact that she was roaming this earth as a troubled soul was part of the reason that she was able to come through so strong.

As they told me more about the case I began to get a stronger picture of what Jacqui was actually like. It was so refreshing to hear details of her life because I didn't want to think of her in the way I had known her for so long; as a tortured soul. I felt I'd made a remarkable bond with her over the years, and felt that if she'd been alive, she would have been the feisty, caring sort of girl I would have liked as a friend.

All too soon, Barbara left and Batters suggested we visit the murder scene. He showed me Ruark's building first, where 'Pokie' had his flat. It felt creepy to stand outside it and know that someone who could behave in such an evil way had lived there. I am sure he thought for years that he had committed the perfect crime. I shivered there in the bright sunshine with the retired policeman.

We then made our way to Jacqui's flat at Lakeside Close, Ruislip. I had never been there before in person, but of course I had in spirit. I stood outside her home and felt an incredible sense of sadness come over me just standing there. The thought that people lived so close to her while she fought for her life made me angry and then sad once more.

He must have been cold blooded to have taken such a chance with so many people living close by. Jacqui was such a beautiful young woman, taken so quickly and violently from this life.

I met Jacqui's family who, though they were still angry at the murder of such a bright young soul, were now relieved that justice had been served. Terry was Jacqui's older brother and it made sense that she should cry out for him in her hour of need. I also met her mother Betty and her sister-in-law Hazel; she had a very nice family. I went to see her grave and put flowers on it. Her grave was like a garden of remembrance, tended with love and attention. Her grave was not a cold place like most; hers was like a little bit of heaven in a corner of a graveyard.

- CHAPTER 13 -

Not only was I in a vacuum during the initial police investigation in relation to what the police thought of my input and what they actually thought of me, I found myself in the same position for many years. It is strange when I think about that time and my sense of urgency to tell the police what had happened because at the same time this need to tell all vied very strongly with my fear that I might not be believed.

Meeting Batters after the trial was, for me, much more than just a walk down memory lane. Yes, it was important for me to see the significant places where it all happened and to meet with a local journalist to hear how the case had been covered, and indeed to be able to rejoice with them at the successful outcome. But much more important for me was when Tony Batters explained it all.

These were not just a simple few words exchanged between friends, with each one saying to the other, 'Yes we did well.' This was far more important, because in talking about the case with him I discovered exactly what he thought about me and my psychic abilities. We did laugh about his first introduction to me and indeed I was quite right about how an English detective might view a psychic, telling him that all her information had come directly from the murder victim, and on top of all that, this psychic was Irish! But I was pleased to see that he had taken me seriously very soon after that. All the little details fell into place for me when I saw those original reports. He was later to admit that the police had received a number of calls from people offering their services as psychics, but that they had all talked nonsense. I was also pleased to see that so much of what I had said was verified.

Tony, as I began to call him, explained that as the first officer on the scene he had stayed at the flat for several hours, taking notes on absolutely everything he saw, from the position of the body, the visible injuries on the deceased, the positioning of the furniture in the room, to the trivial details of the surroundings. He told me in order to get a feel for the crime it is vital that they do this. He went on to explain that after him, a group of Scene of Crime Officers carried out a minute examination of the scene, seeking out trace evidence such as hairs, foot marks, tool marks, semen, saliva or nails. In fact, anything that is alien to the scene is logged and labelled, or attached to exhibit cards, which are also labelled. All of this then, he told me, was brought to the lab, where the forensic scientists took over. Batters quickly went over the post mortem with me as he could see I already knew the grim details. When the police examined Jacqui's nails, they had found minute particles of skin. These were eventually discovered to match 'Pokie' Ruark's DNA. A minute examination of Jacqui's clothes also yielded valuable forensic evidence. He described how his boss had set up an incident room and surrounded himself with experienced detectives he knew he could rely on, but that despite the meticulous cross-referencing of witness statements and alibis, it had been extremely frustrating to find that they just couldn't find a big enough hole in Ruark's alibi to nail him once and for all.

The actual meeting with me, documented in full, made fascinating reading, and as I looked at it, the memories of that time came flooding back to me.

I had initially told the police that I was speaking on behalf of Jacqui Hunt, not Poole. This was of course verified to be her maiden name, which had not been made known.

I recalled that I had told the officers Jacqui should not have been there that night, and that there were two coffee cups in the otherwise clean kitchen. The police, on entering the flat, had indeed found two cups in the immaculate kitchen. On further investigation, they discovered that two men had called earlier to bring her to work. She had been due to start work as a barmaid in Whispers Nightclub in Chesham. As I had mentioned, she wasn't feeling well and decided to stay at home.

One thing that proved inaccurate was that I had said the murder took place on Saturday night, when in fact it had been a Friday night. I remember at the time that Jacqui had said it was a Saturday, so maybe she had been mixed up due to the horrifying stress of what had happened. Batter's notes showed that Jacqui's schedule for both the Friday and Saturday were identical, so maybe she had been mistaken.

My account of letting the killer in was shown to be correct. She thought he had a message for her because her boyfriend's father, George Lee Senior, had also visited earlier that evening to make travel arrangements to visit his son in a detention centre the following week. I didn't know the difference between a detention centre and a prison back then, which is why I called it the 'Nick'. The police presumed Jacqui also thought Ruark may have had a message for her.

I had pointed out that Jacqui knew the killer socially, but that he had become a pest. When the police investigated, they found out that Jacqui and her boyfriend had frequented the Windmill Pub, the same as Ruark and his girlfriend Sarah, and they often drank together as part of a larger group. A close friend of Jacqui's told police that she had informed her of her rejection of Ruark's constant advances when George Lee, Jacqui's boyfriend, was in custody. A man matching Ruark's description had also been seen hanging around the greengrocer's shop where Jacqui worked on the day of the murder, and earlier that week. George's father, who was acting as a sort of protector towards Jacqui, had told police he thought Jacqui had wanted to tell him something earlier in the evening, but had changed her mind. Thinking back, I had told the police that Jacqui had visited her boyfriend in the 'Nick' two weeks before she was murdered. This turned out to be correct. She had visited him 12 days before the murder, and she came to me exactly two weeks after that.

Jacqui had repeatedly called out for someone called Terry. The police knew this was Jacqui's brother.

The jewellery Jacqui had shown me was also missing. There were many more corroborating facts. I had told the police Jacqui suffered from depression and was thinking about her husband. The police had found a prescription for medication in her handbag, and discovered that her divorce was imminent.

I had also mentioned that Jacqui worked in different bars around Hillingdon. It turned out that she worked in pubs in Hillingdon and Ruislip.

I remembered mentioning someone called Barbara Stone but then getting confused because there was no more information. Batters told me that every one of Jacqui's known acquaintances had been contacted but that there was no sign of a woman with that name. But after the second trial, he had asked Terry if he knew who she was. It turned out that Barbara Stone had been a close friend of Jacqui's, but had been killed in a car accident a year before the murder.

I had also told the police that Jacqui showed me where she lived, and I remember describing two blocks of flats and the name starting with an L and ending with Close. Jacqui, it turned out, lived in a block of flats at Lakeside Close. The parking area also matched my description. I had also told them the killer had been there before and had done a job for Jacqui. Police found out that Ruark had visited once before in October 1982, and had switched the electricity mains back on for her after they went out. It was chilling to find out that Ruark had turned off the electricity himself, either before or after the attack, as a part of his plan to kill her or as a macabre parting gesture. I recalled then how Jacqui had first made contact with me by turning the lights on and off.

Apart from the layout of the kitchen, my description of the scene after the murder was 100% accurate, I was told. Batters had been there for five hours after the murder and had taken note of everything, and could not get over how accurate my description was.

I was right about the newspaper lying unread in the hall and the signs of disturbance found in the lounge. I remember Jacqui had kept drawing me towards the bathroom, and it was here where 'Pokie' had attacked her. There was an upturned rug and a broken rail, just as I had witnessed when Jacqui had been thrown around the room. The police report stated that this damage occurred after 8 pm on the Friday evening; the night of the murder. Straight after that Jacqui had drawn my attention to the living room, where I felt she was dragged. This was proved correct too.

I grimaced when I recalled the very personal details I had given to the police about the attack on Jacqui, which proved beyond any doubt that I had to have witnessed it in some way. The final image of Jacqui being murdered, with the cord around her neck, came back to me in a flash, but Batters didn't dwell on this.

He reminded me of how I had told him that Jacqui had sworn a lot when describing the events to me, and told me that the police had found out from her friends that this was one of her noticeable mannerisms when angry. So too was her misspelling of things like names and addresses, as I had seen with the spelling of Ickenham.

I didn't need to look at the newspapers to see a picture of 'Pokie' Ruark because I had always known what he looked like. Batters confirmed that my description had been very accurate. He was indeed of a mixed-race complexion with wavy Afro hair, he was 22 and he was a Taurus. His height of 5'8-ish was accurate, as was the mention of tattoos.

He was an active criminal, involved in burglary and stealing cars. His only legitimate trade, as a plasterer, was learned in prison. He had worked for two days the week before the murder, but had since falsely reported himself as sick. This all fitted what I had said. He was handy with cars, being a DIY mechanic, he was local, and the police had indeed spoken to him already.

I had mentioned that Ruark had been drinking locally the night before the murder, and he had been, in the Windmill, with the other regulars. I instantly recalled telling the police that they were close, and had the right group of people.

I was correct about Ruark's girlfriend, who was a small and pretty brunette. It turned out that Ruark had been in need of money. He was due to become engaged and had promised her an engagement ring, which never materialised. I instantly got a flashback to the image of Ruark trying to take the rings from Jacqui's fingers as she lay dead on the floor. I remember at the time feeling that the killer was a particularly cold person for having done that, and knew he had felt nothing while walking away from the scene of the crime. I had told the police that his friends would be surprised and shocked that he could do something like this. As it turns out, straight after the brutal assault and murder of Jacqui, Ruark had gone home and changed before spending the rest of that night with his girlfriend and other friends at Amaretto's night club. They described him as completely normal and relaxed. All of his friends considered him completely incapable of violent crime.

There were so many minor details I gave that I could hardly remember them all, but Batters had noted everything and reminded me of their accuracy. I had mentioned how Jacqui had changed twice, finally into jeans and a jumper, and these were the clothes she was found in.

There was the mention of an insurance claim. After Ruark was arrested, he was charged and convicted of numerous other crimes including one in which he falsely reported a burglary at his own flat. He had sold the goods on and claimed the insurance.

Then there were the names Sylvia, Betty, and Gloria, and somebody living above the newsagent. Sylvia was George Lee Seniors' wife. Betty was Jacqui's mother. Jacqui had a very close friend named Gloria Robbins, who lived above a newsagent in South Harrow, and who provided the police with a lot of personal information about Jacqui. While at the crime scene, the phone had rung three times and Batters had answered each call. The three people who had phoned were Sylvia, Betty and Gloria.

I could see in Batters' report that my offer to write the name of the killer while in a trance confused him, but again, I was grateful that he had let me do it. Apparently, I held the pad and started to scribble in one area of the page, before moving to another, finally writing one word very slowly and jerkily. I had written the three words that were supposed to tell where the jewellery was hidden, but I could see the confusion that I had had over the name of the murderer himself. Previously, when Jacqui had been calling his name, I had thought she said 'Porkie' or

'Poker', but I remember looking at the page and seeing the name 'Pokie'. Batters had made a note that the handwriting was not mine.

In all, of the 130 pieces of information I gave to the police, Batters told me that 120 were proved to be correct, and that the other ten couldn't be proven either way. I wasn't surprised because I had the closest witness to the crime speaking through me and showing me everything that had happened: the victim. But I was happy to have been of such help. I had named the killer, and given a detailed description of what he had done and how he had done it. The police just couldn't prove it at the time. All those years later, with the advances made in forensics, science finally caught up with the psychic world and the killer was brought to justice.

- CHAPTER 14 -

As a result of the huge media interest both in England and at home in Ireland in the Jacqui Poole story, I was invited to speak on radio and TV. I went on the Joe Duffy Radio Show on national radio and afterwards had people ringing me up and wanting to book me into hotels all over the country, but I was more into the personal one-to-one meeting with people, so I declined these big events. I like dealing with people on a more personal level. Duffy was very pleasant and open and it was through his show that I was invited on to *The Late Late Show*, Ireland's flagship chat show.

I was invited to appear as a guest in November 2001 with Batters. The murder that involved myself as the Irish medium who had helped get a conviction against Anthony 'Pokie' Ruark, resulting in a life sentence being handed down at the Old

Bailey was the obvious topic for conversation that night. Pat Kenny was intrigued with the case and asked both Batters and myself many questions. Batters was able to tell Pat, our host, 'I've accepted the fact that Jacqui communicated with Christine,' and he subsequently informed the highly respected psychical researchers, Montague Keen and Guy Lyon Playfair, that all of his police colleagues with whom he had discussed the case agreed with that interpretation.

It was wonderful for me to hear those words spoken on live television, validating my life, all that I had been through with this case, and everything I believed in, particularly on such a high profile TV programme in Ireland. The police did not normally come out with this type of statement, and the fact that Batters did, was an indication of exactly how much he believed in what I had done.

He informed the audience of the sheer volume of information I had given them that proved to be correct. Only one piece of information was shown to be wrong; when Jacqui spoke of being murdered on Saturday night, while in fact the murder was committed on Friday night. I remember at the time saying that I could only relate what Jacqui had told me to tell the police, and explaining my assumption that she must have got the day wrong by mistake. This was understandable of course, considering what she had just gone through. Batters reiterated that he had been impressed with my abilities even though 'Pokie' Ruark remained free for 17 years.

Batters explained to the audience that it had obviously not come out in court that Jacqui had communicated with me, because as was explained to me, ghosts can't testify. After the show I was inundated with even more calls from every corner of the country. Suddenly, I was like some sort of celebrity. I remained in the studio for a time afterwards, where the interest in my gift was exceptional. *The Late Late Show* got a phenomenal response that week. Their phones did not stop ringing until 3 am that morning. The lines were busy for weeks afterwards; such was the interest in the Jacqui Poole story.

The media interest went into overdrive after *The Late Late Show*. I was invited to appear on *This Morning,* with Fern Britton and Phillip Schofield. *The Richard and Judy Show* were very keen to interview me and Spanish radio and Canadian TV also expressed interest in knowing more about my story. BBC TV also said they would be interested in making a documentary. I was asked to give advice on how the police and mediums work together, to help script writers in their efforts to create good drama. It was all a bit strange for me. For years I had struggled to maintain my integrity and self-belief and was always very conscious of the fact that people looked at psychics and mediums in a certain way, and now it seemed like the world was ready to embrace me and take everything I said to heart. Needless to say, I wasn't used to the attention.

Interest is one thing but when it comes to the Japanese, not only were they interested in my story, they sent a film crew from Paris and Holland over to Stradbally in October 2004 to make a short dramatised version of the story. They presented me with a copy of the film, which I cherish. The amazing story of Jacqui Poole has not lost any of its momentum and remains a case study well known to all psychics, and it is still covered extensively by the media. The Discovery Channel made a documentary which was screened in 2006 on Canadian TV, and this too has generated interest. Once more, the story is fascinating audiences and showing that truth can certainly be stranger than fiction.

THINGS LOOK TO be settling down again now and I am looking forward to living my life in the quiet little town where I grew up, surrounded by so many memories. It has been a long and difficult journey since Jacqui entered my life, and even before that, but it had been one that I believe I was meant to take. The whole story of Jacqui Poole's murder was never easy for me, and at times was downright traumatic, but in the end, I was glad to have been involved because the outcome restored a lot of my faith in my ability, not only to see what others cannot see, but also to help people when they are most in need, and when nobody else can help. I am just glad that Jacqui has finally found peace and 'Pokie' Ruark has been brought to justice, and that that part of my life has now finally been brought to a close.

There was so much pain, and there have been so many times when I couldn't help but feel that I had let Jacqui down, but I prefer to look back over my story and leave it with a vision I hold close to my heart; that of my waking early one morning and seeing the most wondrously intense light, and the beautiful, young Jacqui floating over my bed with the most radiant, blissful smile on her face as she drifted off to find eternal peace. I no longer have to hope that she is at peace, because I know she is.

❧ ❧ ❧ ❧ ❧

I believe angels come to rescue you to bring you to a better, safer place when you die in tragic circumstances. I also believe Archangel Michael helped Jacqui and brought her on the rest of her journey. These rescue angels have continued to play a large role in my life. The role of these rescue angels is unique.

Mediums, psychics and healers all work through love and healing. Mediums send out light and love into the universe when they mediate and generate positive energy. They help to make it a more bearable place for the rest of us. Every Thursday I have my angel night. I light candles, burn incense and oils and invite Archangel Michael, my spirit guide and my other angels to come and pray with me. I pray for people's intentions and I find it very uplifting, and when I flag a little my angels fill me with positive energy so I can intercede on behalf of others. Where I am now is the result of years of learning and hard earned experience. The way I approach helping someone is so far removed from my time as a teenager, when I was so timid and nervous of my gift. I had not developed my psychic abilities and had not grown sufficiently as a person and felt unworthy. My life has been a progression of spiritual growth and understanding.

A guardian angel, once placed by God, stands over, loves and protects their charge from all evil from the moment of conception, through their lifetime up to and including the moment of their death. However, we all have free will and some will choose the path of darkness and evil. The love that a guardian angel has for us is impossible to quantify and understand. They never judge us no matter what we do.

I had heard about the rescue angel but never thought that I could have a role to play with it. I have learned that in all things there must be a balance; this is the way of the universe. Where there is good, there is also evil. For all of those whose choice is evil, there are those who devote their lives to conquer and overcome evil. Over the years I have reconnected spiritually with the angels. There is so much darkness in the world and now, more than ever, there is a need for people to join the invisible army struggling to keep the balance.

Our guardian angels and the host of other angels who populate our world and beyond—holy people, psychics and mediums, our loved ones who have gone before us—are all part of this invisible army. By telling you about a psychic dream I had I can share an experience that gave me a deeper understanding of the battle that continues between good and evil.

All psychics can identify with the fact that many uninvited intrusions can come into your life and for us it is more normal and acceptable. I had a most unusual intrusion one day when my mobile phone rang and I answered it thinking it was a call for me. All I could hear was what seemed to be the news. I tried to hang up but my phone would not end the call. This continued for a time until I realised that the news I kept hearing was about the death of a criminal. This had been broadcast over the media and was part of most conversations at the time. Eventually it stopped and I got on with my work.

I had been meditating and praying as usual that night before sleep. What I dreamt that night will stay with me forever. The difference between a psychic dream and an ordinary one is that in a psychic dream the images remain clear, whereas my mind has no memory of the normal dreams in the morning.

In my dream I was transported into a place like a hall or corridor, not very bright, it was dimly lit. In front of me were three men, one on his own whom I recognised, as he had recently passed over in tragic and violent circumstances. The other two were on their knees with their heads bent low. Their deaths had been well reported and I was familiar with the details of their lives and deaths. What you have to understand is that when someone who has lived on the dark side in life passes over, they can be caught between two worlds.

The angels are there to protect and deliver the souls of those who have departed this life to the light. The devil, however, comes to collect those who he believes are his, because those who deal in evil on earth have to pay the price. Mediums are called on to help guardian angels to help save souls. It is a little like the emergency room in a hospital and the doctor is called in to assist the patient. In my dream I was called in without warning and I had to help the angels save this soul.

The most recent man who died was standing there, frozen to the spot and terrified. I spoke to him and explained to him that he must turn towards the light and move on. 'I can't,' he said, 'I am afraid to move because I have blood on my hands and the life I lived was really bad.' The sense of evil was present and very strong, the devil was there claiming his own, he was fighting for this soul. The angels were there also fighting for him, they would never desert him. I could feel the presence of evil, yet I was protected from seeing the devil as the angels gathered around us. The young man was full of remorse and felt that he did not deserve forgiveness. I spoke to him and told him that he had died as he had lived. He was judging himself now much harder than any Court of Law, but it was not in his power to change anything he had done on earth.

I encouraged him to move on and he took a step, then looked back at the other men and asked why they weren't moving. He said he knew them and they were as bad as him. I explained that it was his time to move on and they were stuck. He looked towards the light and moved. Suddenly the others saw him move forward, which gave them the strength to move after him to where family members and friends were waiting for them. We have to remember that there is never abandonment where God is concerned. No matter what we think of these people who act like this during life, they do need prayers and the light to help them on their journey.

As a result of my involvement in the Jacqui Poole case, I still get many enquiries from people all over the world. One of the more recent has come from Chicago, looking for my help in a murder investigation. I believe that Jacqui Poole's murder was a terrible crime, and the longer I live the more I realise that what happened that particular weekend in Ruislip in 1983 was, in fact, a rescue mission by her guardian angel, who summoned mine. Today I see the entire event as an acknowledgement of my special gift.

- AFTERWORD -

by Montague Keen

READERS WHO MAY be incredulous at the account of Christine's messages from the murdered Jacqui Poole may do well to reflect on the fact that, when all normal explanations have been exhausted, we are left only with the paranormal.

There are certain features of Christine's experience that make it unique. It is by no means the first time that a Medium had helped the police to track down a missing person. Accounts from many countries, and over a long period, testify to this, although each case is controversial and all generate heated arguments about the accuracy of the Medium's statements, the extent to which they were helpful to the police, the source from which the evidence might have been derived quite normally, or the honesty of the parties concerned. But what makes this episode of outstanding interest, and importance, is that a critical scrutiny of all the evidence appears to eliminate every feasible explanation, other than that it was indeed the voice of none other than the

161

dead woman, desperate that her brutal killer should not escape justice, which assailed the young and frightened trainee medium in her lodgings over the weekend of 11 February 1983.

Along with the distinguished author and paranormal investigator Guy Lyon Playfair, whose many books on the subject testify to his expertise as a witness and his experience in probing the improbable, I was concerned to assess evidence from the four principal witnesses. It was, comfortably, the most straightforward and uncomplicated task I have ever encountered. Thanks to the meticulous records kept by Tony Batters, the supporting confirmation of the dramatic interview with Christine by the detective working as Tony Batters' partner, and the vivid recollection by Christine herself of the events of that weekend and the succeeding days, the task of ascertaining all the facts was simple although, as can be seen from our account published in the *Journal of the Society for Psychical Research* in January 2004, it was essential to check every possible way in which Christine, consciously or otherwise, might have obtained the information which proved so evidential.

It is an unfortunate aspect of our legal system that evidence from ghosts is not admissible, since there are not many of them who appear to be susceptible to cross examination. Had it been otherwise, the impatient spirit of Jacqui Poole might not have had to endure the elapse of some 18 years before her assailant was sent down for life at the Old Bailey.

So why is Christine's experience so important? Well, scientists who have devoted years looking for hard evidence that we have souls that survive bodily death, and are sometimes able to communicate with us, have provided a mass of cases which strongly suggest that information, usually coming from Mediums, could not have been known to the Medium. In nearly all such cases, it has been argued that the Medium might have been reading someone else's mind, even when no one alive at that time had the information.

Far-fetched though it might appear, the contention is that the medium might somehow envisaged the moment when the missing or dead person to which the communication referred, and whose 'hiding place' had been known only to the deceased and the killer, was discovered. After all, so the argument goes, we do know that people occasionally foresee a future event. Likewise we have ample evidence of the frequency with which telepathy occurs.

What is more, further evidence shows in what form and how often some mediums quite unconsciously draw in memories from the recesses of the minds of other people, and not merely those in the same room. Add to this the occasions on which glimpses of future events are vouchsafed to receptive individuals (precognition) along with images of distant scenes (clairvoyance) and, lo and behold you have a combination of psychic talents to explain almost anything. Mind you, there is no actual evidence that anyone can operate such a range of psychic faculties, but since all of these component parts are known to exist, who can say that they are never somehow combined? So why assume the dead can speak to us when there's a simpler explanation, one less offensive to orthodox conviction?

What possible evidence, then, could persuade the sceptical that this explanation simply won't do? Well, the most impressive would be precisely what Christine Holohan has provided: facts known only to the dead communicator. Certainly, a goodly proportion could have been culled from the mind of Tony Batters or via clairvoyance from his notebooks, and other bits might have been derived from a local newspaper report or even from mutual acquaintances, had she known Jacqui herself and mixed with her set of friends, and / or patronised her local pub (as to none of which is there a hint of evidence). Even so, we are still left with a residue which baffles and perplexes the critic determined on using any argument to show that something so self-evidently impossible must somehow or other have 'normal' explanations.

How, for example, did Christine refer to Jacqui Hunt when the victim's maiden name had not been published, or mention the fact that she was still going through divorce proceedings when all her friends believed her to be already divorced? More to the point, how could she have known about Jacqui's dead friend, Barbara Stone, whose identity was not revealed for another 18 years, or indicate on a scribbled notepad when in semi-trance the location that a great many years later was found to correspond precisely with the murderer's route home and the most likely location of the stashed-away jewellery? And from whose mind would she have extracted information about the sort of shop over which a close friend lived?

To those outside the coterie of experts in this field, it may not be in the least apparent why Christine's experience is so important, indeed historic, and why this young woman was fortunate to have her developing psychic faculties open to the unexpected and unwanted attention of a desperate soul seeking justice for her killer.

It was a classic case of the drop-in communicator. Usually such spirits display themselves and hawk their grievances by simply dropping in to some innocent circle of friends who are holding séances in the privacy of their homes, not for gain or glory or even experiment, but to see whether they can communicate with their loved ones. The drop-ins are always unexpected, and normally a nuisance if they persist in barging in. On occasions they give information about themselves, and on rarer occasions spell out their grievances. The more detail they give about themselves, and the more difficult it is to confirm the accuracy of the information, the more impressive the evidence that the knowledge was unlikely to have come from the long-forgotten memory of one of the sitters.

To take a thoroughly researched example which, from an evidential viewpoint, ranks as one of the most impressive; that of Runki's missing leg. An entity that made a nuisance of himself by constantly interrupting the activities of a domestic circle in Iceland in 1937 was eventually persuaded either to leave them alone or to give information about himself. Initially he had confined himself to accusing one of the men who had joined the group of harbouring the communicator's missing leg, an accusation which baffled the recipient. Eventually he gave the required information about himself.

The detail was impressive. He described how he had left the house during the night of a great storm the previous century, had too much to drink, taken a short cut across the sands, fallen asleep on a rock, was encircled by the tide and drowned. His body had been eaten by dogs and ravens, and all but one of his bones found on the shore was buried in the local graveyard, which he named. Only the thigh bone was missing. It was later washed up on the beach and buried in a wall in the house of the newcomer to the circle. This somewhat improbable narrative was supported by a wealth of specific information about his name, age, home address, etc. It eventually transpired that the bone, which Icelandic custom forbade anyone from throwing away, but which could not be buried without an indication of ownership, had indeed been concealed inside one of the walls of a house owned by the bewildered séance participant. It was not discovered until 1940, a good 60 years after the fatal storm. It was given a Christian burial, and Runki's spirit was at last at peace.

Even with such a formidable array of evidence that no member of the circle could have known about Runki and his thigh bone, the case does not match up to the evidential level achieved by Christine's experience. Unlikely though it may seem, there was opportunity for the medium involved to have quietly undertaken the research which eventually confirmed virtually all the details given through him by the ostensible Runki. In other words, all the information conveyed was somewhere or other available, and might have been acquired, if not surreptitiously by the medium, then by telepathy or clairvoyance from various records and elderly inhabitants. Not so with Christine and Jacqui. Only the dead woman could have conveyed some of the evidence surrounding her murder and her assailant. Not even if she had been able to read the mind of the murderer could she have divined that Jacqui had changed her dress twice that day, or was expecting visitors to take her to a new part-time job, or was on medication.

In this field there is no such thing as absolute proof. That is the province of mathematics, and even here all mathematics is based on arbitrarily given axioms, such as the assumption that the shortest distance between two points in a straight line. Without that, the entire structure of Euclidean geometry we learned at school would crumble.

In looking at the evidence to answer the question: can we survive bodily death as intelligent personalities able to communicate to those on earth? The answer must be simply that the probability that we do outweighs all alternative explanations.

And for a world which is still locked within the narrow walls of a philosophy that denies the existence of consciousness, that sees nothing in life beyond mortal flesh and blood, that discerns neither purpose nor plan behind our existence, and looks upon the soul as a figment of man's hopes rather than as a demonstrable fact, the traumatic communication which Holohan experienced immediately after the brutal murder of Jacqueline Poole is as profound and important a contribution to the repudiation of that philosophy as any piece of evidence in modern times.

December 2003

Montague Keen is secretary of the Survival Research Committee of the Society for Psychical Research, of which he has been a member for nearly 60 years. He writes in a personal capacity, since the Society has no collective opinions.

- POSTSCRIPT -

THE FOLLOWING ARE extracts from correspondence between Detective Tony Batters of the British Police, and Montague Keen, respected researcher into psychic phenomena, from October 2002. Keen wrote to Batters with a series of questions it seems, which Batters takes in turn to answer. These questions and the information given by Detective Batters throws light onto a lot of the case and gives insight into some of what transpired at the Old Bailey, as well as during the original investigation.

Sent: 11 October 2002 18.48
Subject: Re: Poole murder queries Reply 1
Keen: Was the body discovered only on Sunday, two days after the murder (and by whom?) what was the reason for the discovery delay, especially with a woman with a wide circle of friends, and who was presumably

expected to work at the new pub the following evening?

Batters: You may see a copy of my ordinal police statement, which shows almost all of the following. My answer(s) may contain more detail than specified by the question. This may be necessary to achieve the points you may actually be seeking, but it could become more arduous that answering verbally.

Body discovered by me on Sun. 13.2.83, at approx. 12.50pm.
Father of George Lee had called at her flat at noon, to take her to visit his son in Huntercoombe House (Borstal). They had fortnightly passes to visit Sundays. He was the last person to see her, that being Fri, 11.2 at 8.05 pm, when he had called to make arrangements for that visit. On Sunday 13, he attended Ruislip police station, The Oaks Ruislip, at 12.20pm, having failed to get a reply at the address. After he had expressed his concerns to Insp. Bernard Tighe, Mr Tighe called me to deal with him.
His concerns were that:

• She had failed to answer her phone the previous day and on that morning she did not answer the door
• There were two days' milk on the doorstep

- newspapers were visible through the glazed door
- the curtains were drawn during daylight
- she was in love with his son, had kept all previous appointments, and had enthused about the impending visit.
- when he visited her on Friday, she told him about the depression and reasons for it, including her imminent risk of eviction. He voiced the possibility that she had killed herself.

I went with him to her flat and noted the above. On entering the rear garden, we saw that something was pushing the closed lounge curtains against the window, 6 inches about the lounge floor level. George Lee stated that this was inconsistent with her keeping everything meticulously clean and in place. I broke in. Within minutes of my finding the body, I answered tel.3 calls from:

- Betty Hunt, Jackie Poole's mother
- Gloria Robbins, her close friend/ confidante
- Sylvia Lee, wife of George Lee Senior

Nobody else rang in the entire five hours I was there. Betty Hunt and Gloria Robbins had been regularly ringing since Friday evening and customarily spoke to her daily, at least by phone. None of these were due to visit her.

Gloria knew that on Fri and Sat, Jackie Poole would be working daytime at the Greengrocers, and evening at *Whispers* in Chesham. She would not, therefore, have been alarmed by the lack of contact. However, Jackie Poole's mother Betty was frantic, because she had arranged Jackie Poole's temp barmaid job at *Whispers*, who had rung her to find out why Jackie Poole did not answer her door Friday, or turn up Saturday.

I thought it interesting that Christine appears to mention the three who rang me at the scene, viz. Betty, Sylvia, and 'someone who lives above a newsagents' (Gloria).

Keen: When was Christine's message to the police first recorded?

Batters: I do not know. From recollection, her message was No.115 for the Operation. The Old Bailey Prosecution had the index cards, in which her details were registered re Psychic Input and all the messages. However, I think we saw her on Thursday 17. Andy told me a few months ago that he thought earlier. Her message, which I recall to the effect 'I may have information about the Jackie Poole murder' was received either one or two days beforehand. I believe she told us that she initially telephoned a police officer she vaguely knew, to ask what she should do about the messages she was receiving. He reportedly told her to ring Ruislip police station. It may be important to note that a Major Incident team will not disclose info to a non-team officer, and any who contacted one for information would be refused, his details taken, and his interest investigated.

Shall study the other questions when the chance arises.

Tony

Sent: 11 October 2002 21.24
Subject Re: Poole murder queries

Keen: What amount of publicity would have been available at or before the time when Christine telephoned the police? Was it only after an appeal for witnesses? And when did that take place? Can we identify the precise pieces of information which were by then in the public domain?

Batters: It is a shame I do not have access to all the records kept, which included a book into which any relevant newspaper cuttings were glued. They are still preserved with the case papers. Daily, an officer was sent to the newsagents to buy every national and local newspaper available—for me and two others to peruse. The point of the practice concerns the interviewing of possible suspects, and any claim they might make that their knowledge of the case was obtained from the media. However, TV was not watched routinely, and if a suspect or witness claims to have learnt from that source, TV companies are contacted.

I recall only two or possibly three articles published during the week commencing 14.2.83, each very brief. Det. Supt Tony Lundy was extremely restrictive in the release of information, which referred, as I recall it, to *25-year-old barmaid Jacqueline Poole being found 'murdered' in her Ruislip flat,* which one mentioned *was close to Lido.* The fact that she had been robbed of jewellery was included. It got very little space indeed, expect in the *Uxbridge Gazette.* A large article, with pics (proud neighbour pointing to flat), but very little info about the incident. You could speak to their reporter Barbara Fisher, who has good knowledge of the case and the paper's records.

From day two, the squad had 30+ officers, who circulated amongst all hostelries in Ruislip, Northwood, Hillington and Uxbridge, asking for people who knew her to come forward. However, news of the murder would have spread very quickly amongst her contacts, commencing pm on 13. Every pub, including The Viking in South Ruislip where I think Christine worked would have known about it soon, so Christine could have talked to customers. Say 20% of her 'knowledge' could have come from that source, but uninformed opinion would similarly have supplied her with nonsense. One would also not expect her Viking customers to frequent The Windmill, and vice versa.

Keen: Did the two friends who called at around 7.45 on the evening of the murder, Friday, confirm that Jacqui did not open the door to them but retained the chain on the door, and that she said she felt unwell?

Batters: No. They were not friends of Jackie Poole's, but one knew her mother. Their statements show that they knocked repeatedly, and left without getting any answer. They would not know of the door chain. They were intending to take her to Whispers night club in Chesham to work that evening as a barmaid due to their temp staff shortage.

Meanwhile Lee Senior was indoors with Jackie, having just called to confirm arrangements for Sunday's visit to Lee Junior, and was in any event her 'minder'. When he heard the knocking, Jackie told him to ignore it until they went away. Her health at the time is confirmed by Lee and one other. When he left at 8.05pm, he heard her put the chain on the door, as was her usual practice.

Lee knew Jackie well, and was privy to certain info about the murder which

Christine also revealed. He could have told her, but in addition to the impracticalities and improbabilities, she knew info that he did not. Eg, Christine mentioned Jackie going through a divorce. Lee believed Jackie had already been divorced for a year. The disclosures to Christine, if 'terrestrial', would have required rapid collusion between many people who were not friends.

Keen: Since Christine lived in the same area two miles from the victim, what are the chances that she would have encountered Jacqui and / or some of the suspects, but retained no conscious memory of such encounters, recollecting them by hyperaesthesia (an unusual increased or altered sensitivity to sensory stimuli) subsequently?

Batters: Small point, but distance between homes= 3 miles+.
It is possible that Christine had conscious and / or unconscious recollections. One might argue that the areas they frequented and / or their contacts and lifestyles were too socially / geographically unmatched. I think anyone who shopped in Ruislip would remember Jackie if they saw her at the greengrocers. V. attractive, with most noticeable jewellery. I know nothing of hyperaesthesia.

Keen: How far distant from Windmill pub from Trevor Crescent in Ruislip where Christine lived?

Batters: Two miles.

Keen: It is not clear what further information was given to your colleagues by Christine during (one?) subsequent interview (and when did it (they) take place)? Was further information relevant to the murderer or deceased forthcoming?

Batters: That is because no documentation survived for reference. Following Andy's and my verbal briefing of Det Supt Lundy, other officers were sent to visit her. How many and how often? I do not know, but I know that one tape-recorded interview took place on Mon 22 Feb. On that day, a Squad member returned to my office with the tape, and with the document on which Christine had written whilst 'in trance' in presence of Andy and myself the previous week, and which I (and you) still have.

In Sept 01 after the trial, by chance, I met former lab officer during investigation. He mentioned that he had been one of Christine's subsequent interviewing officers. He may have been present for the tape recorded interview.

Sent: 13 October 2002 00.34
Subject: Re: Poole murder queries
Keen: Do we take it that 'Bird' is slang for a detention centre; and was it your impression that Christine did not know that difference between Bird and (the) Nick?

Batters: Not quite, and I have to admit that the possible significance of the subtle correction was first noticed by Andy. 'Nick' is a precise term for the prison of police custody. The correction seems to be her pointing out that George Junior was not in either. Did she (Jackie) realize she had just said something imprecise to people who would have recognise the point?

'Bird' is a more generic term equivalent to serving any custodial sentence, and lacks the precision of 'nick'. This would include prison, borstal, young offenders' institute, reform centre-or anywhere else offenders get caged.

Christine seems to uses an extraordinary amendment, which we did not discuss with her at the time. I raised the matter with her when we met some weeks after the trial, but she seemed clueless as to my point. I believe she has no knowledge of the criminal process.

Keen: Is the evidence of a close friend of Jackie's about Pokie's attempts to flirt with her part of the trial evidence, and available from its records?

Batters: Yes, from memory, the observation came from a read statement of a witness.

Keen: Did *Tshe Times* reference to an ex-lover derive from what was alleged by prosecuting or defending counsel?

Batters: I have not seen *The Times'* article, but Ruark claimed at the trial that he had been a secret lover-in an attempt to justify the presence of his DNA. He claimed having sex with her twice, once two weeks before, but at a time when we were able to prove he was at a football match. He also claimed to have had sex with her on the evening of the murder. Tony

Sent: 13 October 2002 18.16
Subject: Re Poole murder queries- Reply 4
Keen: Is there any evidence that a St Christopher [medal] was among the stolen goods?

Batters: The fact was part of a sequential list complied from info provided by friends and family after the initial list. These were documented evidence. The first list featured only items of major value, eg. bracelets, rings, necklaces. I remember distinctly that the St

Christopher (the only item with a picture thereon) was not mentioned until further enquiries were made during Week two, and the question specifically put to the family.

Keen: How could Jackie's two changes of clothing that evening have been verified at the trial? By whom?

Batters: The Greengrocer, Patel's statement describes what she was wearing when she left work Fri 11th. When Lee Senior arrived at the home at 7.45pm she was wearing a housecoat. Under-clothing unknown. She then changed into blk pullover and blue jeans, in preparation for work at Whispers. As you know, she was complaining of feeling unwell, and seems to have finally decided against going when they called for her. Still wearing same when she was found Sun 13.

Keen: How was it known that at 8pm Jackie was wearing about 12 rings? Was this Lee Senior's evidence? Or that of the two callers: but they didn't enter the flat, did they? Did she always wear 12 rings?

Batters: Yes. Lee. Always wore a 'large number' of rings. One on each finger on both hands. Some with two.
Keen: When was Ruark arrested and

imprisoned for burglary: was it well before the Old Bailey trial?

Batters: Frequently before the murder, within weeks after the murder, and often since.

Keen: Three phone calls were received by you while in Jackie 's flat investigating the murder: was the fact that she was murdered, or was dead, generally known by then to her family? When and by whom was the body discovered?

Batters: See Answers re Q.1. They did not know. I only told Sylvia Jackie was dead. I also asked her to ring Huntercoombe House to get a message to her son that she had arranged to visit would have to be cancelled for reason's of Jackie 's health. I told Gloria and Betty that I was simply investigating a missing person.
Regards,
Tony

Sent: 14 October 2002 10.34
Subject: Re: Poole murder queries- Reply 5
Batters: Addendum to 11: There was no documented mention of the housecoat during the investigation. My first knowledge of it was when Lee Senior told me in Qs I put to him at the Old Bailey. It may well have been disclosed during cross-examination during

the trial. I thought that some of Christine's info many have originated from them, but I satisfied myself that they never had any form of contact with or heard of her.

Keen: What specific (pieces) of evidence were crucial in your view to the eventual conviction, or at least to the decision to charge Pokie with murder? Was it the intensity of the post-interview investigations (which unearthed the incriminating red pullover) which would not have been undertaken without Christine's information? And why was the red pullover kept?

Batters: The crux was the DNA exchanges between the pullover, and hers, as developed in 1999 to 2000 by forensics officers. They gave evidence at the trial. I believe that, in the absence of Christine's timely info and fast reactions by officers, Ruarks's pullover would have been lost to the bin men. Ruark's pullover was the most damning evidence.
Potential exhibits used to be kept indefinitely as in this case. Numerous bags were stored.
Tony

- BUT GHOSTS CAN'T TESTIFY -

by Tony Batters

EXCERPTS FROM DETECTIVE Tony Batters' Article in Police magazine regarding the Jacqui Poole case:
(The article included a picture of Jacqui Poole with the following caption underneath):

> During a trial at the Old Bailey (7 August—23 August 2001), a prosecuting counsel described the brutal murder of 25-year-old Jacqueline Poole. The jury were told that on the evening of 11 February 1983, Anthony James Ruark, known to his friends as 'Pokie', had visited her unexpectedly at her flat in Lakeside Close, Ruislip, in the suburbs of west London. The victim, a greengrocer's assistant, was viciously beaten, sexually assaulted, and strangled with a light-cord. Gold chains, rings and other jewellery, which she was always seen wearing,

were stolen from her body and her home. Police also found the electricity power turned off at the mains. By the year 2000, recent advances in DNA technology had been able to match clues found on her body with the accused. This story concerns one extraordinary aspect about the case which could not be disclosed to the jury.

The article gave an honest account by Detective Batters of his involvement in and opinions of the role played by Christine Holohan in the Jacqueline Poole murder investigation:

'I was a member of the Jackie [sic] Poole Murder Squad throughout the original 15-month investigation. Within a few days of the incident, a colleague and I were assigned to visit 22-year-old Christine Holohan at her council house in South Ruislip, after she had telephoned to offer information. Her call omitted to mention her belief that her source of information was the dead victim. She told us that she had been 'bothered by psychic experiences' since her childhood in Ireland. She denied any personal knowledge of the case, or that she had spoken to anyone connected with it. Only very brief newspaper reports had been publicised. She claimed she was repeatedly hearing the voice of a spirit who called herself 'Jackie Hunt', which was

Jackie Poole's unpublished maiden name. My colleague Andy and I were sceptical at first, but our attitude changed quickly. To describe her as well-briefed would be an understatement. My contemporaneous notes of that interview are still available for independent review.

'In a series of self-induced trances, the young woman gave us extraordinary accurate details about the murder scene, as if she were reading my mind. I had been the first officer on the scene, where I remained for hours. She described the scene just as I found it, including the victim's position, clothing and injuries. In a step-by-step reconstruction of the crime, she relayed a series of events which seemed to match the evidence.

'For example, we initially thought the incident had taken place in the longue, but she insisted it started in the bathroom. There was an overturned rug there, and a towel-rail had been pulled from the wall, later confirmed to us as very recent damage. She knew that in the course of robbing her, the killer had left two of the many rings she always wore. They would not come off.

'Some of the details Christine gave were of trivial nature, like the fact that the victim had just made coffee, the position of some of the crockery in the kitchen, a letter in the lounge, disarranged seat cushions, unread newspapers. It would not have been possible for her to have seen the flat at the time or afterwards, and it would seem unlikely for this sort of detail to be passed on to her by someone else. These could have been guesswork, but she also knew that Jackie was undergoing a divorce, that she was suffering from depression, that she had just been given a prescription by her doctor, that she had not intended to be at home on the evening that she died, but felt unwell, and that two men had called at her door on innocent business, just before her murder. And much more. Were the less important and sometimes irrelevant details given to lend credibility to the more significant issues?

'At one stage, completely out of context, Christine said she was receiving the name "Barbara Stone." We never came across the name during the investigation, and discounted it as someone for us to trace. It was not until the trial, 18 years later, that I learnt she had been a friend of Jackie's, but had been killed in a car accident a year or more before Jackie. She regularly mentioned the name of "Terry" as someone the voice kept asking for. Jackie was a member of a large family, but was closest to her elder brother called Terry.

'Christine was not one hundred percent accurate. For example, she had said that the crime had taken place around 9 pm on Saturday. The time was right but it was Friday. Jackie's body was found on Sunday, the day that Christine claimed the "messages" started. And sometimes the meaning was ambiguous. However, of some 130 points Christine made, more than 120 now seem to have proved absolutely correct. Others could never be proved or disproved.

'In a series of apparent trance, Christine replayed information which she claimed to be receiving psychically. She described the murderer in great detail, his age and month of birth, height, skin and hair colouring, 3 tattoos, and the type of work he did. She mentioned his criminal history, and referred to a recent insurance fraud which he subsequently admitted to us. We were to look for scratches, later attributed by him to a collision with a hedge. He would have had a social connection with the victim through a friend who was in prison, and had visited the address before to perform a task. Indeed he had done—to check the fuse box which he was to switch off during the murder months afterwards. She warned that some of the killer's associates would support his alibi, and that none of them would believe he was capable of violence. Each of these facts applied to the man who has now been convicted.

'On the most important question of them all, the killer's name, the young woman claimed that she could not understand Jackie's reply. "She repeating a word. It's not clear and it doesn't sound like a name. She says she wants to write it down!"

'We asked if she could also find out what happened to Jackie's jewellery. Christine took up a pen and notebook, and seemingly returned to a trance-like state. After a few moments, she began to write. Claiming that she had no control over the pen, she then handed over the notebook to us.

'In addition to some illegible scribble, the words, "Pokie" and "Garden" were written in a crude script. "I thought she was saying Porky or Poker," said Christine, "but it didn't make sense. She kept saying 'garden' when I asked her about the jewellery." This aspect has never been explained satisfactorily.

'Christine used the same page of the notebook to record more information. This time she wrote down the word "Ickeham" and some figures. The only known relevance of Ickeman would seem to involve Pokie's alibi. When asked subsequently to account for every minute of his movements around the time of the murder, Ruark told the police after leaving the pub in Ruislip, his motorcycle ran out of petrol in a nearby village of Ickeman. Apart from a period of 30 minutes, his alibi seemed to be corroborated by his friends at both ends of the journey.

'The officer leading the investigation, Detective Superintendent Tony Lundy, decided to treat Christine's information as if witnesses who wanted to remain anonymous had used her as an intermediary. In essence, that information was simply the hearsay name of a suspect, supported by detail which could validate her source's credibility.

'Pokie had already been interviewed as an acquaintance of the victim, he and his girlfriend having responded to an immediate police appeal. His subsequent arrest resulted from a lie in his witness statement that he was travelling by train at the critical time. New evidence that he was actually using a motorcycle lost value to the fact that he was a disqualified driver. But he was now seen to have had his opportunity, albeit brief.

'The emergence of Christine's information and its unusual nature added focus at the time when suspects were legion. Jackie's garden and another at Pokie's flat were dug up, but without result. Witnesses were interviewed and re-interviewed with regard to his movements on the evening, and during the preceding weeks. Although these enquiries resulted in his being charged with numerous crimes of dishonesty, he maintained his innocence of the murder throughout. Further interrogations were to be conducted months later.

'During the first week, two more sessions were held with Christine, and although the officers reported being impressed by her grasp of related issues, we gained little of consequence. Perhaps we did not ask the right questions? The timing of our first session with her may have been critical to the recovery, from a rubbish bin, of an item of his clothing which became forensically significant to the trial. Moreover, the concentration on his earlier movements produced enough background information to meet any conceivable defence, if more conclusive evidence ever emerged. Eighteen years later, those efforts were to discredit Pokie's last-ditch claim to have left traces of himself at the scene before the murder.

'Almost all that Christine said would have and indeed did come to light during the investigation, but we lacked the vital evidence of witnesses and forensics. Even a televised appeal on *Crimewatch UK* failed to produce any useful leads. Hearsay evidence is not admissible in criminal proceedings, of course, even less so when it comes from the hereafter! Despite our particular interest in him and his dubious alibi, Ruark had at that time to be viewed in the context of a score of possible suspects, several with alibis which could not be corroborated. After fifteen months of further enquiries to trace and eliminate those alternatives, the Squad was disbanded.

'The case was re-opened in 2000, amongst hundreds of other cold cases which were aided by the development of DNA, particularly low Copy Number technology. The findings were completely conclusive, identifying numerous exchanges in bodily fluids, skin cells and clothing fibres between the victim and the killer, Pokie Ruark. Not least significant of these was his DNA under her fingernails. The chances of error were quoted to the court as less than one in one billion. On being told in May 2000 that he was being arrested for the murder of Jacqueline Poole, Ruark coolly asked the arresting officers, 'Who's Jacqueline Poole?'

'During the course of the investigation, we received various calls from people offering their services as psychics, but they talked nonsense. Christine was exceptional. We were never to find the remotest connection between her and anyone who could have told her all that she seemed to know. In theory, and given enough time and recourses, she could have collected much of her information through contact with the actual killer or someone in whom he confided, and with the victim's relatives and friends, and also with the Murder Squad Officers. I collated every statement and document throughout the 1983-4 investigation. However bizarre the conclusion, the only single source of all her knowledge had to be the victim. If any lesson is to be learnt, it is that one should not dismiss the possibilities out of hand.

'On 24 August 2001, Ruark remained impassive as he was convicted of murder by a unanimous jury, and sentenced to life imprisonment. We hope Jackie and her family feel that justice has at last been done.

'Christine returned to Stradbally, Ireland in 1986, and became a professional medium. I retired from the Met. Police in 1992, and head European investigations for a U.S. based company.

Footnote:

'After we were with Christine for about an hour and a half, we were trying to get her to admit being given some information by the victim's family or even a member of the Murder Team. But she insisted that the only source was the voice in her head. As a gesture, she offered to give information about one of us. Andy volunteered. He was asked to hand over something of his own. Christine then described three different aspects of his personal life, none of which I had known about. We had not worked together before.

'The first was extremely personal indeed and quite detailed. He confirmed those details to me after we left. She also stated that he had received a letter concerning "essential electrical work". He told me that he received a mortgage offer from a Building Society the previous day, with the condition that the house he wanted to buy was re-wired. Andy was quite dismissive about the third, which predicted his imminent transfer to another police area. Unexpected to him, maybe, but an order transferring him to another Division came with a few days. He was quite shaken by the whole experience. The Squad included more than twenty detectives, and we ourselves had picked up the assignment only that morning, and by chance.'

Tony Batters, December 2001, in *Police* magazine.

- CASE HISTORIES -

SHIRLEY,
affirmation of Christine, March, 2005.

Christine had been recommended to me and at the time I personally was in a very bad place. She wasn't telling me what I wanted to hear, but some of the things she told me most definitely came to pass. I go to her every year religiously ever since '94. I tend to go January or early February.

I have no doubt that she is a hugely spiritual person. You can feel she definitely has the ability to love unconditionally. She is very caring. She has spoken to me about things over the years. This year she told me of a woman in the spirit world who was a very strong willed person, very glamorous and described how she dressed. She said to me it is Elaine or Eleanor, and that this particular spirit was pushing me to move on, to come into my own power and I didn't know who she was talking about. As I have come to understand Christine you just accept it because it will come out in the wash eventually. It transpires that she was my mother's sister. Her name is Eleanor and she was an incredibly glamorous woman and she apparently is with me at the moment trying to make me come into my own power. It is absolutely fascinating.

Christine can see people who have passed over. She told me a few years ago that she could see a man sitting at a writing desk and he had lots of books around him and that she got the impression he was a writer, now there is no way she could have known that my great grandfather was Oliver St. John Gogarty, the famous writer, but she was seeing him and at the time he was protecting me. He was surrounded by books and writing. At the time she was confused, she was saying I think he is a writer and she got confused but in actual fact he was a writer but he was a Renaissance man, he was also a surgeon, an athlete, he was a lot of things. And I think that was why she was a little confused.

It would have been back in 1998, a long time before she knew anything about me, and it is only in the last couple of years we have known each other. She said to me, 'He is directly related to you,' but I didn't say who he was. I tend not to but I don't think she really cares. I don't think she needs you to validate that. That was years ago.

When years were leaner I can remember her saying, 'Your needs will be met.' She was making it clear I was going to be all right.

Two years ago Christine told me that a friend would die that year. She said, 'You are not very close but you are friends,' but she said it was not family and I couldn't conceive who it would be. She said, 'It's a woman and she is dark haired and she will die after a short illness,' so I put that to the back of my mind. A friend of mine had had cancer and she was in remission for several years but that summer she became quite ill and she was in hospital for two weeks. I drove to Dublin and she died that night.

Once again I find it extraordinary that Christine could see that and even the way she described my relationship with her was spot on. To this day I still question on a spiritual level what was the point of that, why was I the one that was there comforting my friend.

Christine has been insisting a lot recently that my son will do well. He works with his father and Christine has told me he would go into writing and theatre and music and she keeps saying he is more like your father. It hasn't come to pass but he is very young and there is no doubt it will come to pass. She said she is emphatic he is going to be very successful. He is very witty; I can see how it would happen for him. I feel that I am not remotely sceptical and so I don't see it as being an extraordinary thing any more, it is natural and I totally believe.

Nowadays when I go to her it is just really for a bit of guidance, she can give me an insight into what is going on. People go to mediums for something they have not realised. There is an emptiness in their lives. That is one of the benefits of knowing her, when it starts to unfold as she has predicted it is easier to accept it, I am more accepting rather than worrying about whether it is the right thing; if she said it will happen then it will.'

ANN
Premonition of murder

'I first met Christine when I was working as an Air stewardess at RAF Northolt. I had the rank of Cpl., that was when Margaret Thatcher was at the helm. It was an exciting time for me then and in my capacity as Cabin Crew, I met Margaret Thatcher, Prince Philip, The Duke of Edinburgh, Harry Kissinger and many others. Christine and I became firm friends and the fact that she was a medium did not put me off becoming her friend. A lot of other girls at that time would have been in awe of her gift and not so keen to get friendly.

Christine told me that I would move to this cottage with John. She described the lane, the railway line and everything in detail to me. Christine described the cottage, so much that I felt I knew it before I lived in it. She told me it was an old cottage and there was a well somewhere on the property. When we went to view it there was a well in the garden and—what a surprise—it was called Well Cottage. She described a little bridge on the lane. There was a railway line, she could see a train, and she said, 'Your Nan is here'; that was my grandmother.

The lane was very close to the cottage, the minute you came out of the house you could walk down there. It was very convenient and that suited me very much because I had a big golden retriever called Sam, who needed loads of exercise. I had no fear whatsoever until one weekend Christine came to stay. We went for a walk down the lane when all of a sudden she stopped and gave a shudder. One moment we were laughing and joking and the next Christine said that she had a bad feeling. I asked her what was wrong and she replied, 'I sense somebody is going to get murdered here, I've just got this bad feeling.'

It was a lovely summer's day and Christine said, 'Don't risk it any more. I have a feeling going down my spine and I got a premonition that a girl was going to be murdered here. Don't come this way anymore because if anything happens to you, if you get attacked Sam can't help you.' Christine described the whole thing to me. She felt it was my grandmother that was telling her to warn me.

She told me that she had a strange feeling after Jacqui Poole died as if she was trying to tell her how to help people. She described what she thought was a young blonde haired woman walking her dog and as I was blonde and fitted the same description I was frightened. Christine asked me to promise her that I would not go there on my own any more and I didn't.

Within a year a young blonde woman was found suffering from severe head injuries after a savage attack in the very lane exactly where Christine had said it would happen. She died soon afterwards in hospital.

To this day I am eternally grateful to Christine for her timely warning, it could have been me that was murdered. I still keep in touch with Christine and paid her a visit in the summer of 2004.

SALLY
letter of endorsement.

Dear Christine,

It was lovely to finally talk to you on Wednesday. I do hope you book is coming together the way you wish it to be.

Back in the spring of 1984, I came to see you. I did know then that I was going on a trip abroad but I never told you where. You saw that holiday and told me that once I was there, I would keep 'taking my shoes off'. You also saw me wander along what you could only describe as 'corridors under the sea.' Finally, you described an Indian reserve with tippees and Indians. I thought at the time these were the oddest details. What I hadn't known prior to my going to Tahiti to visit my sister, I soon found out once I got there. Before entering any Tahitian house one must always take one's shoes off and line them up neatly outside. A few days into my holidays, my sister arranged for us to visit a Lagoonarium; you walk down into the lagoon through glass-panelled walkways under the ocean, where you can see the beautiful Polynesian fish swimming around you. So, these were the 'corridors under the sea'.

At the end of a busy three weeks, it was time to return. We decided to stop one night in Los Angeles so that our 11-year-old could see Disneyland. It was a rushed one day visit, we didn't see as much as we would have liked but we took a trip on one of those Mississippi steamers; whilst meandering on the waterways, we turned a corner and all of a sudden, on the river bank, there was display of an Indian reserve complete with tippees, life-size models of Indians, etc.

I was rendered breathless at just how accurate you had been when I hadn't known beforehand that I would be experiencing any of these sights. I have never forgotten that reading. On a more personal level, my marriage was in deep trouble at the time. You told me you couldn't see us splitting up at the time and there would be another child. We did make up in and I had another baby. I don't know whether my story can be of any significant contribution to your book but you are very welcome to use it, as it was and still is exactly what happened.

MARY

When our beautiful son died this spring, he took part of our future with him and left behind a lot of broken hearts among his family and friends.

My daughter and I went to see Christine a few months after his death, neither of us had ever been to a psychic medium before but had often heard about Christine. His spirit came through within minutes of Christine closing her eyes and going into a trance. She took on his mannerisms and tone and said, 'Your son is here,' and told of the circumstances of his tragic death and his terrible sorrow, and of the hurt left behind him.

He said to my daughter, 'You were there at my grave last night and you told me to make sure I was here today, I've been waiting with granny.' Christine said he saw me with his red t-shirt, pressed to my face crying, a few days earlier. He talked of and named his lovely girlfriend since their schooldays. He saw one of his best friends leave for Australia six days after his death and spoke of his friend who loved him dearly. Everything was astoundingly accurate. There were loving messages for my husband and other family members, and finally he told Christine of his childhood book that I had given away shortly before his death.

Christine is a remarkable woman, with a wonderful gift of seeing beyond our world. She brought up names, occurrences and details, that are only relevant to our family and friends over the years, and not in your wildest imaginings could Christine previously have known any of this. We were astounded, it left no doubt in our minds that my son was there. Christine is a very genuine and uplifting person with a lovely laugh and with the kindest voice, as she said quietly to him 'I hear you.'

We came out walking on air, so amazed that such things could occur in this sometimes unkind world that stole my son away from us.

❧ ❧ ❧ ❧

KAREN

I first came to hear about Christine after my brother had suddenly gone missing for no apparent reason. He had just disappeared into thin air. Police had been notified and searching had begun.

Christine's name came up several times and eventually we made contact with her. She was such a lovely warm person and made us feel completely at ease with her. She was very calming and reassuring which was what was needed during those very traumatic weeks.

It's only when something like this happens to your own family that you can perhaps try to understand the pain experienced by all those families of missing people. Each time I hear of a person gone missing my stomach still churns and my heart goes out to them and their families.

Christine felt right from the beginning that my brother was dead and that he would be found fairly soon, but we had to use all resources possible including media, newspapers, police etc. She felt he was in water, beside a large motorway and something was connected to the word 'Pass.'

We searched day after day and prayed if not for his safe return but at least to find his body. Everyone was so helpful to us and supportive with all the searching.

After a couple of despairing weeks which none of us could ever forget, the day arrived when his body was found. It was day filled with so many mixed emotions. We were all heartbroken and saddened with the news but deep down we thanked God that at least he was found and we could bury him and visit his grave. His body had been found in a river beside the M11 motorway and a hundred yards from 'Passingford Bridge' just as Christine had said.

Christine and I have remained good friends throughout these past years. She has been a tower of strength to me throughout those dark days and months after his death. She could share with me some of my pain as she had experienced it within her own family.

I treasure her friendship and will always be grateful to her for all her help back then. I was delighted to hear that at long last she has decided to share her experiences with us in her new book. I wish her all happiness in the future.